# The Furniture Fabrication Factory

By

Ken Susnjara

# The Furniture Fabrication Factory

## First Edition

Thermwood Corporation
Old Buffaloville Rd.
Dale, Indiana 47523


© 2000 Thermwood Corporation


Printed in the United States of America
First Edition Printed 2000

ISBN 0-9665693-2-6

# Table of Contents

# Introduction

In my book, "Furniture Manufacturing in the New Millennium", I introduced the concept of "Furniture Fabrication". In Furniture Fabrication, each part of a piece of furniture is produced on a machine, one at a time. As the parts are being machined, the machine operator sands and assembles the final product. When the cycle is complete, an entire piece of furniture has been built.

The technical feasibility of this concept has been demonstrated at several trade shows. Highly sophisticated furniture pieces have been manufactured on a single machine, at these shows. Most furniture people that have seen these demonstrations now agree that technically it is possible, but they generally believe that this concept is not practical for full-scale production.

 I hope that this book will change that attitude.

Furniture Fabrication is not only practical, but it will produce quality furniture with fewer people, at lower cost, in less space with fewer production problems than any system operating today.

I know that these are bold statements. I believe that I can fully support every statement.

In this book I will detail a conceptual design for a Furniture Fabrication Factory. Much of the fundamental thinking is quite different. Everything from material flow to how inventory is grouped and stored is quite different than current practices.

I will also talk about people and management. Just as the technology and manufacturing approach are different, so is the relationship between the various groups in the company. Old fashioned twentieth century management techniques won't work in twenty first century companies.

I would ask that the reader approach this with an open mind. Today, the furniture industry is faced with significant challenges. Furniture manufacturing today is based on manual labor. It is a highly labor intensive business in which automation has simply improved the actual processing functions but has done little to significantly reduce the dependence on low cost, manual labor.

There are two significant labor problems that threaten the very existence of this industry today. First, low cost labor is becoming more and more difficult to obtain in the US. Because of population trends, the number of new workers entering the workforce was projected to decrease through the 1980's. The overall size of the workforce was increasing, but the rate that it was increasing was less and less each year. This should have meant that industries, such as woodworking, would have found it almost impossible to hire new workers by about 1990.

This, of course, didn't happen. The reason was that a large portion of the female population also began to enter the workforce through the 1990's. This did not eliminate the effect of the population trend, it simply postponed it. Now, as we enter the new millennium, the effect is starting to impact us.

It is possible that some other social trend might again, alleviate the impending problem. For example, we might decide to allow a much larger number of immigrants to enter the US. These immigrants might then provide the needed new labor to support current production methods.

Based on current political attitudes, however, it does not appear that this is likely. A major labor crises could change these attitudes. It does not seem prudent, however, to base a company or industry's future on these random attitudes.

At best, labor will be available, but at a higher cost. This brings us to our second fundamental labor problem.

If we are going to use today's labor intensive production methods, it possible to use labor in places where wages are fifty cents a day. Even if these places are a half a world away, it is possible to ship the final product to the US and still be priced well under comparable products made here.

This is a serious problem. If the competitiveness of an industry is based on the cost of labor, the area with the lowest cost labor will win. Our labor cost is going up and theirs is almost free. If something fundamental doesn't change, we will lose.

There are only two possible ways for the US woodworking industry to survive. First, we leave our basic structure and methods essentially unchanged and get our labor cost down to fifty cents a day or so. Since we don't have to ship our product as far, this should give us an advantage.

I can't think of any way to do this. I don't think it is a good idea, even if it could be done. For an economy to prosper and grow, everyone, including all the hourly paid labor needs to prosper and grow. A system where one group profits because another is paid low wages simply doesn't last. History has shown this over and over.

We could try to preserve our inefficient methods by imposing duties and tariffs on the low cost product. In this way we could leave our system in tact and simply charge everyone more for their furniture.

Again, history has shown that nations that have tried to preserve and protect the old through taxes and tariffs have seen their entire standard of living sink as a result. Protectionism in the face of serious economic threats seems, at the time, like a sound approach. When we look back, however, we generally see that these efforts occurred at the beginning of major economic or technological shifts. We also see that it just plain doesn't work, at least I have never found an instance in history where this approach actually worked over any period of time.

The final conclusion is not what most of us want to hear. To survive, we must change our system so that its basic advantage comes, not from cheap labor, but from somewhere else. In the case of the furniture industry today, that "somewhere else" is technology. We do have a technological advantage over "cheap-labor", third-world countries. As an industry we must turn to this technology.

In this book, I hope to show you the kind of technology we have at our disposal. Little of the amazing potential of this commercially available technology has been put to use in the wood industry. The technology that has been used, has generally been used to enhance and improve existing methods. The real potential of this technology, however, is not in improving current methods. Instead, it is in replacing current methods with new, much better approaches.

Unfortunately, "new, much better approaches" are very uncomfortable. In general, the furniture industry has a difficult time making money. Only when everything is working perfectly is a small profit possible. Over the years, managers have learned that any change that might even slightly disrupt the operation could turn that small profit into a large loss.

The industry has been conditioned to take only tiny baby steps. They take extreme care to make sure that they don't stray very far from the "tried and true" methods of yesterday. New technology, which is growing and developing by leaps and bounds, is being incorporated drip by drip.

I fear that a continuation of the current trends will turn the furniture industry into another television industry. This once large, strong, vibrant industry doesn't exist in the US today. If you had talked to management in the television business before it disappeared, they would have assured you that Japan, which is only known for building "cheap plastic toys" couldn't possibly build televisions. There was no reason to panic and change things that work "just fine".

Today, much of the management in the furniture industry think things work "just fine". They acknowledge that they will have to change and grow, but they do not see a revolution coming.

It's coming!

The amount of change that the industry will see is much more significant than anyone realizes. I believe there is still time to revitalize the industry and dominate the world in furniture production. To do this however, requires changes on a level that no one is trying today.

There may be many approaches that will work. In this book, I will detail one approach that I feel can compete with anyone in the world. Since neither I, nor anyone else has tried it on a large commercial scale, much of the discussion is somewhat theoretical. The ideas, however, have been developed by people that are skilled in both high-technology and furniture production. Concepts that we have been unsure of, we put together and tested.

Although the methods, layout and processes are somewhat unconventional, they all work.

Over the years, I have repeatedly heard wood furniture manufacturers complain about their basic raw material, wood. It is inconsistent, it changes size with moisture, it splits, cracks and warps.

I have never heard anyone, however, praise the single biggest benefit of building wood furniture. That benefit is, that the product is made of wood!

The wood may be crushed and pressed in particleboard, sliced into veneer or used a solid wood. It is still wood.

This simple fact is the key to automating furniture production. The final product is essentially made of a single material. Virtually every part of the final product can be processed through the same machines.

Many products today require substantially different processes to manufacture the various components. A television, for example requires electronics, wire, sheet metal, plastic and glass. Totally different machines are used to make the glass tube than are used to roll the sheet metal or mold the plastic.

Those industries that have seen rapid, profitable growth share this important trait. The plastics industry molds parts from plastic. The basic requirements are plastic and a molding machine. They produce a huge variety of finished product. They even use a variety of different plastics, but basically they press plastic into useful shapes.

Semiconductors have been a huge growth industry. They have totally revolutionized mankind. They are basically made of sand. Again, there is a tremendous variety in the final product, the processes and the technology. In the final analysis, however, they are still processing sand.

These examples are industries that have seen huge reductions in labor and have seen tremendous increases in productivity. I have heard that if the automobile experienced the same improvements as the computer chip, it would now travel at over two thousand miles per hour and would cost less than two dollars.

I believe that the singular raw material aspect of a product is a key factor in whether or not it can be automated. Wood furniture has this important characteristic. Theoretically, wood furniture is an ideal candidate for serious productivity improvements.

The words that I have written in this introduction so far are words that I have spoken many times when talking to members of the furniture industry. At this point, they generally conclude that I really don't know the problems associated with the production of wood furniture. I believe that just the opposite is true.

Management in furniture companies are so "shell-shocked" from the day to day battles that they don't see the real potential in what they are doing. As you read this book, I ask that you forget the detail, day to day problems that you are familiar with and look carefully at the underlying concepts. Once you have finished and can see the whole picture, then you can see how the new approach handles all those daily problems.

I believe that the industry that I am trying to sell into is at a crossroad. If it turns one way, it will wither and die. If it turns the other, it will become an exciting and highly-profitable growth industry. I sincerely hope this book helps to move the industry down the better path.

# Chapter 1

## What's the Problem?

# Chapter 1

## What's The Problem?

I have started this chapter by referring to a problem. It is amazing that, even today, there are many managers in US industry that don't see it coming. They don't see a major problem ahead.

In talks with management in the furniture and woodworking industry, I have found that many also don't see a major problem. Of course, there are normal business problems such as competition, difficulty in obtaining quality labor, environmental and governmental regulation. These are the types of problems we have dealt with in the past and we are confident that we will deal with them adequately in the future.

Some managers recognize that the market is somewhat more competitive today than it was a few years ago. The pace seems to picking up and it seems to be more difficult to make a profit. You pretty well have to do everything right to prosper today. I see a lot of people that are within a few years of retirement. Some have told me that if they can just hang on for a few years, doing essentially those things that have worked well in the past, they can leave the future problems to the future managers.

This is somewhat like standing in a street, trying to avoid the cars and bicycles as they pass. What these people don't see is that they are also standing on a railroad track and a freight train is barreling down on them at ninety miles an hour. I am alarmed because most people in our industry don't see it coming. They are not looking in the right direction.

Everybody gives lip service to changing technology and the promise for the future. What they don't see is just how fast these changes are taking place. They don't see how these changes will devastate their industry and they aren't taking the steps necessary to profit from these changes.

The changes are not just technological. Technical changes, primarily in communications, are a major driving factor. Today, because of the Internet, everybody in the world can talk to and understand everybody else without the information being filtered by his or her government. It is no longer possible for an oppressive government to stifle its people by keeping from them the true nature of how everyone else in the world lives. Everybody can see and understand the standard of living in successful nations such as the United States. The television programming you see is essentially seen everywhere in the world.

This communication and the knowledge it brings are creating new demands. These new demands are causing a breakdown in trade barriers between nations. Not only goods, but also capital can today flow between countries as easily as it flows within a country. You can almost instantly invest in bonds or stocks in dozens of countries, many of them third-world underdeveloped countries. Individuals can invest in securities and financial products that were the exclusive prerogative of banks and major financial institutions just a few years ago. This is dramatically changing the world.

These facts are causing all nations that want to participate in the new wealth building to adopt essentially common legal and financial practices. It is also making these nations dependent on each other.

Today it is easy to run factories, or even parts of factories scattered around the world. E-mail, Intranets and video-conferencing make an office or factory, half way around the world, seem like it is right next door. Advanced companies have better, easier communications with operations scattered around the world than some of us have within our own home office.

Changes have happened in the past and industry has adapted to them. I don't believe, however, that the total transformation of the world has ever occurred as fast as it is occurring right now. I am not exaggerating when I predict that we will see more core, fundamental changes, in how industry and finance function, in the next ten years than we have see in the last hundred, maybe two hundred years. Everything is changing, and everything is changing quickly.

In this New World, the consumer will be king. Those companies that can supply and service the customer best will grow and prosper and those that fall short, even a little, will be executed. Your customer will be able to instantly compare what you make with what every one of your competitors makes. EVERY COMPETITOR IN THE WORLD! You can no longer count on the convenience of having your product at their local furniture outlet to generate the sale. They will be able to buy it from almost anywhere and likely at a better price.

Your customers will be able to talk to dozens, hundreds, maybe thousands of your current customers. If current customers have a problem with your product, you will probably not sell any more of it. Today, the potential for that communications already exists, and it is being used, but its use is still somewhat limited. You can still get by with product problems. Within a year or two, any product problem for any company will be common knowledge almost immediately.

It is possible that furniture factories won't even exist as they do today. A furniture company might only sell the design, as a software product, maybe even sold and downloaded off the Net. That design would then be taken to your local fabrication facility where it is loaded into a machine and your furniture is fabricated, much like the local copy shop prints color presentations from your software programs today.

As I ponder wild ideas like these, those of you who know how furniture is actually made can come up with a thousand reasons why it won't work. You can state technical limitation after limitation that would keep this type of system from working. Many of these limitations may actually be valid, but no one is trying to overcome them today. With just a little effort, every reason you can think of can be overcome. Something as wild as this can actually work.

We will not move directly from where we are to a local fabrication shop executing a purchased furniture design. There are some intermediate steps. In fact, if these intermediate steps are not taken, it is possible that furniture won't be built in the U.S. anymore. With the economy becoming more global, production of all goods will move to whatever area of the world can produce them at the lowest cost.

If the basic component of a product is labor, that product will be made wherever the relative cost of labor is cheapest. This may not be the area where the absolute cost of labor is cheapest, especially if some skills are required for the production process. It will not, however, be an area where labor costs are high. Once the basic skills are mastered, being extremely skilled is likely not worth a substantially higher rate of pay. Those areas where the basic production skills can be purchased for the lowest price will be the areas that produce products that are based on labor.

If a product's basic component is technology, it will be produced in an area where the high technology skills and support systems are readily available. It will make no sense to try and produce this type of product in a low labor cost area if extensive labor is not required and the necessary technical skills are missing.

Furniture production, today, is based on labor. The methods that are used are labor intensive and the competitive position of the final product is determined by the cost of the labor. If you double the hourly labor cost of most furniture factories, they could no longer compete and would likely go out of business. This is a sure sign that the product is based on labor.

With a product based on technology, if the base labor rate should double, it would not threaten the existence of the company. It might reduce profits, but it would not make an otherwise competitive product, non-competitive.

Using this criterion, the furniture industry is based on labor. This is a major problem. As I stated earlier, in the New Economic World, products that are based on labor will be produced in areas where labor is less expensive. It does not appear that low cost labor will be a characteristic of the United States. If everything remains unchanged, furniture production will move off shore.

We are already seeing some signs of these forces at work. More and more furniture is being produced in places like China. In the past, the products coming from these areas was pretty much junk. This is not true anymore.

A few months ago, I bought a piece of furniture from a well known, local furniture store. I bought it because I liked it. An American furniture designer, whose work I like, designed it. It was good quality, with good styling, top materials and a well-done finish. It was low cost, but that really didn't figure in the decision. I would have paid considerably more. As you guessed, when I got it home, I discovered it was made in China. Had I known that, I might not have bought it, just because of my personal attitudes. It was, however, a very nice, top quality piece. Those of you that feel that your quality will save you are already in trouble. From personal experience I can assure you, they can make products every bit as good as yours, and at a lot lower cost.

Another sign of impending problems is the availability of labor. Most furniture companies I talk to are having a very difficult time getting the labor they need at anywhere near a cost they can afford. They are seriously discussing or implementing programs to bring workers in from Mexico. This is a sure sign that something is seriously wrong with the core basis of the product. It won't be long before companies figure out that it is even less expensive to simply build furniture in Mexico rather than try and bring the low cost labor to existing factories. Management can either move to Mexico or...

Just listen to the arguments...
*"Furniture is a major industry. It employs a huge segment of the workforce. It is not reasonable to imagine that it will simply move overseas. Sure, they may get a little larger market share, but there will always be enough business left in the US for a core furniture industry"*.

When I first started in business over thirty years ago, I heard these exact same arguments. The large, profitable and growing television industry I was selling to was sure that the US would continue to dominate this new technology and product. It was ridiculous to imagine that the entire industry would be lost, but that is exactly what happened. This happened at a time when there were trade barriers and tariffs to try and protect American industry. Despite these barriers, the business went to Japan.

At one time the US was the largest producer of shoes in the world. It seemed to managers in that large dominant industry that there would always be a core shoe industry in the US. Today, no shoes are manufactured in the US. NONE!

In the past, people believed that trade barriers would protect them. They didn't. Today, even those barriers don't exist. History has shown that they generally don't work, but most people don't really realize is that the US is not even able to impose them if we wanted to. Should we elect to erect trade barriers to protect your industry, the market would punish us severely. Huge foreign holding of US securities would be sold, driving down their price and dramatically raising interest rates in the US. The cost of everything would rise and US products would be much less competitive on the world market. We would be faced with a recession and every industry would suffer to try and protect your business. This simply won't happen today.

We are part of a world financial community. To remain part of that community and enjoy the benefits, we must live by its rules. One of those rules is "no tariffs". There is really nothing to stop the American furniture industry from moving overseas. If we want to have a furniture industry in the US, we will need to change the basis of the industry. If we try and keep it as a labor based business, we will surely go the way of the television and shoe industries.

This book is my attempt to show that there is a way of fundamentally changing the industry. There is a way to change it from a labor based business to a technology based business. I believe there is a way to produce furniture at a substantially lower cost, using substantially fewer people. We can compete and that's the good news.

The bad news is that I don't see any way of evolving from where we are today to the new structure. The two are so totally different that they are incompatible. The new structure needs to be started from scratch. Most of the methods, most of the equipment and most of the investment we have made cannot be used in the new structure.

This almost looks like an answer that is not really an answer. Most companies will feel that it is ridiculous to consider throwing away everything you have worked for and starting over. From today's perspective, I have to agree.

I can offer two answers. First, by the nature of the new structure, it is possible to start small. You can develop small, low volume operations. You can develop the technology, analyze the results and refine the process. This can be done, even while you continue to struggle with the current problems.

Once you know the new systems work and what the results really are, you then have a viable direction should you be faced with the intense competition I believe is coming.

My second answer is that, if I am right, things will get so bad, so quickly that this solution will not look nearly as radical as it might look right now. Most of us have lived during an era of rock solid stability by historical standards. The changes we have seen, while they may appear dramatic to us, have occurred slowly by historical standards. I don't think the changes that are coming will be nearly as pleasant.

There is another possibility that we should consider. In the past, when major changes overran an existing industry, outsiders brought about those changes. Many times the existing market leaders turned down the new ideas, only to be crushed by those same ideas. Hewlett Packard turned down the Personal Computer because the idea of having computers in the home was ridiculous. IBM gave the DOS operating system to an upstart called Microsoft because everyone knows that the real money is made in hardware, not software.

I have already been approached by a group of young entrepreneurs who were trying to revolutionize the furniture industry. They wanted to sell furniture on the Internet through a high traffic site and then build it in modern new factories. We developed a concept where a central rough mill supplied material "kits" to regional factories that built furniture using the concepts I will explain in this book. The idea would have worked great and they went out looking for venture capital.

Unfortunately, they got caught up with some traditional furniture people that convinced them that the "old ways" are best. At that point, much of the cost and logistical advantages were lost. This left only the advantage of selling over the Internet. I doubt they will get the required funding and if they do, they will be just as vulnerable as the rest of us to foreign manufacturers who, by the way, also use the Internet.

These people knew nothing about furniture, and yet, they came very close to creating a revolution. As the global world dawns and all industries are up for grabs, outsiders will seriously look at our industry. Until now, furniture companies could feel somewhat safe just because of the barriers to entry. To run a furniture company, you needed a factory full of different machines and skilled people to set-up and run those machines. You needed sales outlets and distribution systems. It was not possible to simply step into the industry and become a major player overnight.

Those barriers are disappearing. Today you can build furniture on a single machine with some hand tools. My company has been demonstrating this at trade shows for over a year now. At one Atlanta IWF show we completely manufactured three different pieces of complex, high-end solid wood furniture in a forty by sixty foot show booth. It would require over $1.5 million in traditional woodworking machines to build the same pieces. Sure, the bigger investment would result in more volume, but the barrier to building your first piece no longer exists, and with the same investment you can build volume furniture at a substantially lower cost.

This same thing is true when it comes to selling. Traditionally it required years of work and a multitude of personal relationships to develop and refine an effective sales and distribution system. The industry relied on formal markets, distributors and local furniture stores to move their product. This is also changing.

Today, anyone with a little knowledge and a few hundred bucks can enter the electronic marketplace. The Internet is the great leveler. A customer can't tell how big or how old a company is by looking at their web site. Furniture, along with everything else is being sold over the net. The mark up that the retail store normally received is now being used to ship and service the product as well as offering a lower price. The furniture store may very well run into the same problems that the bookstores are running into today.

At the time this book is being written, only a couple of hundred million dollars worth of furniture has been sold over the net. But, that is up from zero a couple of years ago. At the current growth rate, it is estimated that half the purchases in the US will be made over the net in five years. There is no reason to believe that the furniture industry will be the only industry exempt from this trend.

When I have told various managers from the industry about this they almost always counter with a litany of reasons why this won't work. People want to see what they are buying. They want local delivery. They want to deal with a store that can handle problems should they arise.

To understand these arguments you must understand human nature. When a person is faced with a personal tragedy, the doctor telling you that you have an incurable disease for example, they go through several well documented stages. The first stage is denial. You don't believe him. You get a second opinion, then a third. It just can't be true. This is followed by anger, depression and eventually acceptance.

When we are faced with tragic or unacceptable news in the business world, we go through these same stages. The normal reaction of everyone that is told that the world they know is coming to an end and is being replaced by a different one is denial. It just can't be true.

It is normal to conjure up a host of reasons why it can't be true. This may actually be your reaction to the things I will discuss in this book.

Unfortunately, just like most those told they have an incurable disease, it is true. It is important for you to recognize the reaction you are having to these new, and uncomfortable, ideas and force yourself through the stages to the acceptance stage. It is only at that point that you begin doing the things necessary to deal with the new reality. Until then you are being swept by events outside of your control and are simply denying them rather than reacting to them.

Our world will change dramatically. The furniture industry will also change. Maintaining the current course will not work. Your business will fundamentally change, there is no question about that. The only question is whether or not you will get in front of those changes and profit from them. The other alternative is that the change will overwhelm and destroy your business as others take advantage of the change. What you do today will determine which result you will experience.

There will be many, many ways to profit from the chaos. What I hope to offer in the remainder of this book are some core technologies that can provide a tool that can compete on a world wide scale. None of us can see exactly how these things will play out. In the final analysis however, everything can't be done on the Internet. Someone will still have to build the products. In the end, I believe all of us, even manufacturers, will become service companies. The service we perform will be making a product for our customer, but we will operate much more like a custom service company than a traditional manufacturing company.

In this environment, a solid, competitive, flexible manufacturing system will be vital. I believe the ideas that I will present to you in this book will offer the foundation for this new system. I can't possibly give you every answer but I can give you some insight that will allow you to find those answers.

As I develop these concepts and designs, I know that we will encounter many areas that have not been tried before. Rather than simply leaving these to question, I intend to try each and every concept. If I say you can change from one product to another quickly, I will show you exactly how to do it and I will be able to tell you exactly how fast is "quickly" in minutes. Thermwood is certainly not in a position to set up an entire factory along these lines. At the same time, we are in a position to test and demonstrate every major function of that factory. I hope that much of the remainder of this book will contain the insights we learn as we attempt to put these theories into practice.

Before we start, let me share some goals with you. We would like to achieve as close to $1 million in product sales for each production employee as possible. I don't know how much you produce per employee, but I believe that this represents an 80 to 90% reduction in labor from most furniture companies today. We would like to be able to produce furniture in batches of one with no financial penalty. If possible, we would like to be able to customize the furniture for each customer. We would like to make the factory easy enough to run that it can operate twenty-four hours a day with little problem. We would like to operate the factory with little or no middle management. We want to know exactly what is happening at any time and we want to be automatically notified of any problem as soon as it occurs so we don't have to constantly watch everything. We want every person in the factory to have instant direct access to every other person in the factory.

Can we really do all this? I think so. As you read the remainder of this book, I will show you how it can be accomplished and I will share with you the problems and pitfalls of making each and every part of it work.

# Chapter 2

## Nested Based Manufacturing

# Chapter 2

## Nested Based Manufacturing

As this book is being written, the fist step toward full furniture fabrication is already entering the industry. This approach has become known as nested based manufacturing.

Nested based manufacturing simply means that a variety of parts are nested on a sheet of plywood, particleboard or MDF and then those parts are cut out, normally using a CNC router. Although this approach has been used to make upholstered frames for some time, the real use of the term began with the kitchen cabinet industry.

Kitchen cabinets, especially custom kitchen cabinets face some unique problems. Each kitchen produced represents a single, special design. Although the cabinets are built using more or less standard construction practices, sizes and configuration of each product is unique.

Because of this unique nature, most kitchen cabinets, even today, are still cut and built by hand one at a time. A series of products, however, have been developed to try and automate this process.

Cabinet design software packages were introduced to simplify the initial design effort. Once it became possible to design the cabinets on a computer, it also became possible to automatically break down the cabinet designs into the individual components. It was now possible to create a cabinet design and then obtain, from the software, a detailed dimensioned print of each of the parts needed to build the cabinet.

Now, full sheets of material could be cut up into the individual parts. The next step, of course, was to have the computer decide how to nest the parts on the sheet of material to offer the best yield. Now, not only did the computer design the cabinets and make prints of each part, but it also showed you how to cut the individual parts from the full sheet of material.

The next step was obvious. Once the computer could nest the parts, instead of providing you with cutting instructions, it could simply write a CNC program for a panel saw that would automatically cut the full sheet up into the individual part blanks.

At about this same time, another new piece of equipment was gaining popularity. This machine was first called the point-to-point boring machine. Its primary purpose was to bore holes, both horizontally and vertically. These machines were also fitted with routing heads and saws and manufacturers began calling them machining centers or panel processing centers.

These machines originated in Europe where 32mm dowel construction was common. Cabinet manufacturers discovered that if they teamed a point to point machine with a panel saw, they could produce an entire kitchen cabinet. The panel saw would cut out the blank, which was then drilled on the point to point machine. The cabinet could then be assembled using dowels and adhesive or KD hardware.

It didn't take long before the design software created the CNC programs for the point to point as well as for the panel saw. Finally, there was a fully automatic system for handling custom cabinets. The approach became quite popular, but there were problems.

Although the use of a panel saw and point to point proliferated rapidly, the problems kept this approach from becoming the predominant method of building cabinets.

The first problem was based on the fact that cabinets made this way required that they be assembled using dowels. Without commenting on whether it is accurate or not, a large portion of the cabinet industry did not feel that dowel construction was as good as standard dado or mortise and tenon construction. This portion of the industry were simply unwilling to embrace the point to point simply because they were unwilling to switch to dowel assembly methods.

Because of the nature of how point to point machines work, the overall production speed was not as great an improvement as you might expect. While the machine moved rather quickly and could generally drill multiple holes at one time, the real Achilles heel was setup.

Point to point machines typically used a series of vacuum pods to hold the part in place for machining. Most parts were held in place by several pods that were located under the part in locations where there were no cuts or holes.

As each panel was brought to the point to point machine, the vacuum pods needed to be set up in the proper locations under the part. Then the correct program for this part must be located and loaded. Then the blank must be properly oriented and the cycle can be started. Once the cycle was complete, the process must then be repeated for each different size part.

As you can see, the machine operator must be technically qualified. Even then, errors were quite easy to make. It has been common to drill into or route through vacuum pods which were incorrectly located. Wrong programs and wrong orientation can also result in scrap.

Despite the difficulties, many companies successfully operated these systems, but then a new approach appeared. The basis for this new approach was a vacuum hold down system that we call Universal Vacuum.

This approach originated in the late 1970s in the aerospace industry. The aircraft companies were faced with the need to hold down sheets of aluminum, which were to be cut up into individual parts. These parts were computer nested so no two cycles were the same.

The original approach for holding these parts was to create tabs on each part to hold it in place. An automatic screwdriver drove screws into locations on an aluminum sheet that would later become the tabs. The sheets were screwed to a plywood table and then cut out, cutting around each tab that was being held by a screw. After the cut cycle, the screwdriver would go back and unscrew all the tabs. When the parts were removed, the tabs were cut off using a pair of tin snips and the parts were complete. You can see why they needed a new method.

Their new approach used a balsa wood table. The table was made of glued up blocks of balsa wood with the end grain facing up. Balsa wood has a characteristic that air can flow easily through the end grain but will not leak through the cross grain.

This balsa wood table was placed over a vacuum plenum and a high volume source of vacuum added. This was the first universal vacuum table.

By the mid-eighties, Thermwood decided to experiment with these methods for holding wood panels. While the balsa table worked very well, it was much too expensive for the wood products industry. We tried a variety of different materials until we discovered that certain types of particleboard worked almost as well as balsa at a fraction of the cost. Thermwood's Universal Vacuum system was created.

We then built a CNC router we called the Panel Processing Machine. It was to compete with the point to point machines. One of its major features was the new Universal Vacuum table.

We set up the system at a dealer in North Carolina and invited dozens of furniture companies to come and see our new offering. They came and they saw.

We never did sell many panel processing machines, but within a month of our show, universal vacuum tables could be seen in virtually every furniture company that visited us.

Now, almost fifteen years later, this hold down method is used by almost everybody and has become the basis of a new approach called nested based manufacturing.

Universal vacuum has the advantage that it can hold virtually any sized part and it does not require setup. A full sheet of material can be laid down, held by vacuum and a group of nested parts cut from the sheet. A new sheet can then be laid down and a different set of nested parts cut from that sheet.

It now makes sense to machine the parts in a single cycle, on a CNC router, versus cutting the sheets up using a panel saw and then moving to a point to point machine. This approach is what has become known as nested based manufacturing.

The only process that cannot be completed easily using this approach is horizontal edge boring. Edge boring, however, is only needed for dowel construction and dowel construction was only adopted so that we could use point to point machines. With today's nested based manufacturing, we can use or return to using dado or mortise and tenon construction methods.

If you actually want to use dowel construction, there are a couple of methods that will work. The most obvious is to simply drill the horizontal holes off-line in a secondary operation. While this can work, the locations of the holes is important to the accuracy of the final assembly. If you do not locate the parts properly, the final cabinet can be off.

Another approach, available from Thermwood, involves drilling the horizontal holes when machining the back side of the parts. To understand this we must understand Thermwood's approach to cabinet construction.

In designing our nested based cabinet systems, we opted for a traditional mortise and tenon construction method. This provides strong, very accurate mortise and tenon fits between the parts, but does require that certain parts be machined from both sides. This is actually not as difficult as it sounds.

The process starts with machining from the front side using programs automatically created by a kitchen design software package. Labels are printed for each part in the nest. Those parts that require back machining have a bar code printed on the label. To machine the back, the operator simply scans the bar code, which loads the correct program. The part is then positioned against a fixed fence and the start button is pressed.

At this point, the entire edge is open, so if horizontal drilling is required it can be done at this time.

There is one other consideration that I should explain. One reason that point to point machines use vacuum pods instead of Universal vacuum is that it raises the part so that the body of the horizontal drill can pass below the bottom of the part without hitting the tabletop. You need to allow clearance for the drill body under the part.

With Universal Vacuum the part is lying flat on the tabletop so how do you allow clearance for the drill body? You don't.

To perform horizontal drilling on a universal vacuum table, Thermwood has developed and patented a low profile horizontal drill. With normal drill construction, a bearing or bushing around the horizontal drill shaft raises the shaft too high and causes clearance problems. These problems are increased when the bearing or bushing is pressed into a housing.

To get around this problem, Thermwood made the entire drill body from bushing material. This allows the horizontal drill shaft to be located right at the bottom of the drill body. It can drill a horizontal hole in the center of a ¾ inch panel lying flat on the tabletop.

Now that this is said, with nested based manufacturing I feel it is better to use true mortise and tenon construction methods. I believe they offer a better quality cabinet then 32mm dowel construction and they have a major advantage over typical dado construction.

Many cabinetmakers build cabinets using dado construction. They use a panel ( ½ inch for example ) and dado it into a second panel using a ½ inch bit. Although this sounds easy and straightforward, there are some major difficulties possible.

The source of these difficulties is that a ½ inch panel is not a half inch and a half inch bit is not a half inch. Both are close, but close doesn't always work.

If the panel is five or ten thousandths oversize and the bit is two to three thousandths undersize, the parts won't fit together. If the panel is undersize and the bit oversize, the parts will be too loose. Using a simple dado construction and a fixed bit width relies on tolerances that are outside your control and sooner or later it won't work very well.

With mortise and tenon construction, both the width of the mortise and the width of the tenon are machined. The mortise hole is cut using an undersized bit. One side of the hole is cut then the bit is shifted over and the other side cut. This assures that the width of the mortise is machined exactly the same each time.

These cuts are made using a control feature called tool radius compensation. When the router bit is changed, the diameter of the new bit is measured with a micrometer and input into the control. The system then compensates for the new tool diameter assuring that every mortise is cut accurately. This accuracy is much tighter than the normal commercial diameter tolerance of router bits.

The same thing occurs for the tenon. It is cut using the bottom of a router bit. The tool length is also adjusted using another control feature called tool length compensation. An optional feature called automatic tool length measurement can measure the exact tool length and input this number into the tool table within the control, assuring exact tenon dimensions.

Using these features, every mortise and tenon fits properly regardless of the diameter of the mortise tool or the thickness of the panel.

One other trick that some of our customers use is to cut the tenon using a tool that has a five degree taper on the bottom. This cuts tapered tenons. When this tenon is inserted and clamped in place, it wedges into position and offers relatively secure connection. It is normally possible to apply adhesive to the joint, clamp the cabinet in place and then remove the cabinet from the case clamp. The wedged joints hold the cabinet together while the glue dries, eliminating the need for a large number of case clamps, staples or screws.

Now that we have covered some of the construction methods, realize that nested based manufacturing can support virtually any cabinet construction method. There are a number of KD fastening systems for cabinets that can be incorporated into nested based methods.

A real advantage of nested based manufacturing of cabinets is that virtually any construction method can be supported at lower cost with faster production rates.

How does nested based manufacturing fit with furniture fabrication? Nested based manufacturing is actually furniture fabrication if the entire piece of furniture is made of panel stock. Although this is the case for some kitchen cabinets, most furniture is a combination of panels and hardwood components.

True furniture fabrication must be able to process both the panels and the hardwood components during the production cycle. Nested based manufacturing is actually part of furniture fabrication when you are building case goods or similar products that use panel stock.

Nested based manufacturing for kitchen cabinets, as it exists while this book is being written, addresses building only the cabinet box itself. Some cabinets also use hardwood face frames and five piece raised panel doors. Producing not only the cabinets, but also the face frames and doors, is full furniture fabrication. These same techniques can be used for building almost any piece of case goods furniture.

Thermwood has developed a system for producing not only the nested based cabinet boxes but also the hardwood face frames and five piece doors. This system demonstrates many techniques that also apply to case goods furniture production. It is likely that in the future, other companies will offer their own approaches to producing these components.

In the Thermwood cabinet system, the programs necessary for producing the nested based boxes as well as the face frames and doors are all developed from the database of the cabinet design software. The actual CNC programs are created by an automatic CAM system. In the chapter on programming, I will explain in detail how a typical CAM system works, however, in this case all the CAM and Post Processor functions occur completely automatically in a couple of seconds by simply pressing a button.

This fast programming system is important in cabinet building, since each kitchen design is a unique set of programs. The same software and automatic CAM capabilities can be used to create programs for case goods, however, these programs may then be run over and over again.

A major goal of Thermwood's face frame and door system is to process material in the most basic form possible, eliminating as many preprocessing steps as possible. For this reason, the incoming stock is generally random lengths of stock that has been planed to thickness and ripped to a fixed width. If companies wish to mold shapes into some of the edges to eliminate processing steps, the system will accommodate that but, it is generally not necessary and pre molding will not generally improve the production rate or costs significantly, if at all.

A key requirement for the hardwood processing capability is a second router with a horizontal adaptor. To this is attached a saw blade with a router bit sticking out through the center of the saw blade. Although this is sort of an odd arrangement, its purpose will soon be seen.

In addition to the horizontal router, an extruded aluminum clamp system is used. This clamp uses an expanding rubber hose much like a bladder press to clamp the material in place.

To understand how this system works, let us go through the construction of a typical face frame and door. We will start with the face frame.

The program has been completed and networked to the machine control. The program for the face frame is loaded and the start button is pressed. The machine head moves to position the saw blade into the frame holding fixture. It is located about 24 inches from the front of the table and the saw blade is not running.

The control now tells you to position face frame stock against the saw blade. These instructions are audio. Since the cell operator doesn't really know what he or she is producing, these instructions are quite important.

You push the material against the saw blade, activate the clamp and press the start button.

The machine now moves the stock under the saw blade, turns on the saw and cuts off the stock to the proper length. The main router now turns on and machines the necessary mortise slots to fit the face tenon in the cabinet box. The stopped saw is then positioned off the back of the machine table.

The control now tells you to rotate the part 90 degrees and place it against the saw stop.

You move the part to the back, position it against the saw and activate the clamp. You then press the start button.

The main router now machines the deep mortise holes to accept the cross pieces.

If necessary, it also machines a tenon off the end of the part using the router bit that projects from the center of the saw.

If a tenon is needed on the other end of the part, the control will instruct you to flip the part and position it against the saw once again.

As you can see, the machine operator works in conjunction with the control and the machine to measure, cut and machine the parts. The cell operator must simply follow the verbal instructions from the control. When all the pieces have been machined, they fit together into a face frame that magically snaps into the face of the cabinet.

This interactive operation with the machine is new to the industry. There have been programs that required the operator to reposition parts, however, this application is different. Past programs were fixed. That is, each time the program was run, the operator performed exactly the same motions in exactly the same sequence.

In this system, the operator is constantly following instructions, however, there is no repeating pattern. Each time, the sequence may be different. Most of the time the operator isn't quite sure what part he or she is actually making. The machine control handles all dimensions, measuring and cycle sequence. The operator simply follows instructions and out comes finished parts ready to assemble.

This offers some major advantages. First, a less skilled operator can run the cell. The operator no longer needs to work with dimensions. The operator does not need to read prints or read, interpret and follow written instructions. The operator does not need to read a tape measure or make dimensions judgments.

Another advantage is that it is faster. All this reading, understanding and measuring takes time. Sometimes it takes a lot of time. The new methods eliminate all that time and thus produce more parts per day.

Five-piece doors are produced in essentially the same manner.

I have discussed the details of this system to try and show the type of thinking and processing that is required for full furniture fabrication. By combining the techniques for building a cabinet box with the techniques for making wood face frames and doors, most case goods can be built. These designs can then be enhanced and modified by adding design treatment, carvings and other detail to the basic structure.

Nested based manufacturing is showing the way toward full furniture fabrication. We already have customers that purchased a cabinet package using that package to build bedroom furniture. It also dramatically demonstrates that full custom products can be efficiently built using this technique. Latter in this book I will discuss mass customization. When you encounter this concept, remember that as impossible as it sounds, it is already being offered in another segment of the industry, nested based kitchen cabinets.

# Chapter 3

## The Layout

# Chapter 3

## The Layout

We will now try and develop a basic factory structure and layout. In this effort we will try and develop a design that offers the potential for major cost savings. To begin we will start with a blank piece of paper, or a blank computer screen for those who are more enlightened.

The basic concept for this new factory was first introduced in my book "Furniture Manufacturing in the New Millennium". I called this idea "Furniture Fabrication" and essentially it relies on a cell, which can build an entire piece of furniture.

This Furniture Fabrication Cell uses a sophisticated, multi-function CNC machine to perform the machining tasks. It also includes one or more manual machines that each perform one specific task. The machine operator not only runs the machine but also sands and assembles the furniture piece in the cell.

A key ingredient of this cell is the ability for an ordinary operator to change from making one piece of furniture to making another in just a few minutes without the need for outside help.

At this point, a lot of questions come up. Can this really be done? Is it technically possible to make an entire piece of furniture on one machine? It is cost effective? The answer to all these questions is yes, but I would like to defer a more detailed discussion of these important points until later in the book where I can give each area the complete analysis it deserves. Until then, I would like to explore the ramifications as if these things really could happen.

A good place to begin is to try and determine exactly where the savings are going to come from. We plan to approach the problem from a different direction, but it will help if we can see how the different direction will result in lower costs.

Let's start with labor. We are going to try and reduce the number of people required to operate the factory. Where is this labor reduction going to come from?

To answer that question, let us look at a typical furniture factory. The exercise that I am going to describe is one that I have actually performed. Go into your plant and examine, really examine, the individual, specific functions that your employees perform. Divide every action into one of two categories, useful or useless.

Useful actions are those that add value to the part or product being built. Useless functions are those that do not physically change the product in any way. You may believe that some useless functions are required in order to perform useful work, for example, moving a part to a machine may be required before the machine can perform useful work on the part. The fact is however, the useless work does not change the value of the part and if a way could be found to eliminate it, the part value would not be reduced.

As an example of this concept, let us classify the various tasks required to drill a hole in a part. Bringing the skid of parts to the drill machine is useless. Picking up a part is useless and putting it in the machine is useless. Actually drilling the hole is useful, since it changes the part and thus adds value to it. Removing the part from the machine is useless and moving the skid of finished parts away is also useless.

If you use this classification system, most furniture factories have between 90 and 95% useless work. Almost all labor in today's furniture factories does not add value to the final product.

This comes as a great surprise to most and many simply won't believe it. It is true and this basic fact is a cornerstone to the new structure that I will develop.

If you still can't accept this, I suggest that you go into your factory and watch your operation with a critical eye. Don't rationalize that useless labor is needed to support the useful labor, but simply see if the motions your people are doing are really increasing the value of your parts.

It is quite easy to see that the industry does not understand this concept, just by looking at areas that it focuses on for productivity improvement. Furniture companies and machine vendors are all concentrating on making the 5 to 10% of labor actually doing useful work even more efficient.

The real potential for revolutionizing the industry is in eliminating the 90 to 95% of the labor that is doing useless work. Because the industry is concentrating solely on the actual production effort, any technique that eliminates useless labor by slightly increasing the amount of useful labor is automatically discarded. This is true even if overall labor costs drop dramatically.

For our effort here, we will focus on the total labor requirement, and not fixate on any one area at the exclusion of others.

Another area where significant savings are possible is in inventory investment. The typical furniture factory has an inventory of raw material, in-process inventory, stored between production centers, and finished goods. The raw material is being stored at the lowest overall value per part. The money tied up in raw material is simply the cost of the material plus the cost to unload it and place it in its storage position. As the material sits there, its cost actually increases because there is an ongoing cost for the warehouse space, which, it theory, should be borne by the materials stored in that warehouse.

Finished goods are being stored at the highest cost. The money tied up in finished goods is not only the cost of the raw materials in those pieces, but also the cost of all the labor and overhead that were expended in producing those pieces. Again, the ongoing cost of the finished goods warehouse continuously increases the cost of the goods stored in it.

In-process inventory exists at a variety of costs. Parts that have only been partially completed may have a value near the raw material value. Parts that are ready to assemble may have a high value because they have absorbed costs associated with each of the production centers.

Just as with raw materials and finished goods, in-process parts continuously increase in cost as they absorb the overhead costs of the buildings in which they are stored.

This discussion of inventory costs is being conducted on a theoretical basis. It applies accepted accounting standards, but on a mico-managed scale. I do not believe that any real accounting system can keep tract of these exact costs of individual parts. Nonetheless, if we are going to understand how to get these costs down, we must examine them in this type of theoretical detail.

The key point to this inventory discussion is that it requires money to maintain the various inventories. There is a cost associated with tying money up. If you need to borrow the money, the cost is the interest you must pay. If you use your own money, the cost is the interest you would otherwise get by investing the money in an interest bearing account.

These facts are the basis for "just in time" inventory management. Through proper planning and scheduling, raw material inventory is maintained at a very low level. Raw materials are received as they are needed and spend very little time on the shelf.

This same thing can work for finished goods. Product is not actually built until just before it must ship. It is built and then quickly shipped. Again it spends little time in the warehouse.

The result of these efforts is that the investment needed to maintain a raw material and finished good inventory is reduced dramatically. The downside, however, is that the manufacturing operation is much more sensitive to problems. If a material shipment needed this afternoon does not show up this morning, a whole line of product may not get produced properly. Also, there is very little time to develop an alternate course of action.

In a typical factory, 90% of the parts may be processed and waiting in in-process inventory because 10% has not shown up when it should have. In this case, raw material inventory is kept low but at the cost of higher in-process inventory. Since in-process inventory is stored at a higher value than raw material, a few supply problems can derail an otherwise good plan.

In our new factory structure, we are going to attack the cost of inventory from three directions. First, we are going to essentially eliminate in-process inventory. Material will go from the raw material state to finished goods in a matter of an hour or less. While, in some cases such as carvings, there will be some in-process inventory, the level will be a tiny fraction of what is required in most factories.

We should be able to operate an effective "just in time" program associated with raw materials. We should also be able to do this without the dangers normally associated with this type of program.

The Furniture Fabrication Cells that we are basing our factory on can switch from making one product to making another in literally a couple of minutes. Since there is no in-process inventory, once a piece is complete, it really doesn't matter what the next piece is. If material didn't show up for the piece you want to produce next, you can simply make something else until the material does show up.

Also, because there is no advantage to producing furniture in batches, you can produce exactly what you need to ship, reducing finished goods inventory dramatically.

From an inventory standpoint, our factory should be able to operate with a minimum of raw material, virtually no in-process and a minimum of finished goods.

In addition to these two major cost areas, labor and inventory investment, there are a variety of other costs that this new structure can minimize or eliminate.

Set-up labor for machines is included with the labor savings but the parts that are scrapped during the set-up represent some real savings. It normally requires a few test parts each time a machine is set up. If machines are changed over a lot, in an effort to reduce inventory, running smaller batches result and the value of scrapped set-up test parts can become significant.

Management and scheduling costs should be substantially less in our new structure. It is not too difficult to schedule product through one machine. It is even easier if every machine can make every product. This is highly flexible factory and the more flexible and responsive the factory, the easier it is to schedule and manage.

Scrap should be less. Today, if a machine setup is wrong, it is likely that an entire batch of parts will be scrapped. Companies go to great lengths and establish elaborate, and expensive, quality control procedures. Even with this extra expense, batches are scrapped in every factory.

Current woodworking machine tools are analog. This is, they are set up using adjustment bolts and slides that can be set at an infinite number of positions. This means that the position of any machine adjustment must be checked to make sure it is within acceptable tolerance. Setting these adjustments and checking the resulting part is a specialized, skilled job. A human error in this area results in expensive scrap or rework.

People can and do make mistakes. Any system that relies on human judgement will eventually fall victim to human weakness. Most factories have to strike a balance between the cost of the quality system versus the cost of the resulting scrap.

The Furniture Fabrication Cell, however, is digital. There are no analog settings to adjust. Any measurement that is required is accomplished automatically by the machine. The chances of scrap are reduced dramatically simply because human judgement is removed from the process. The only possibility is that the machine itself malfunctions.

Unfortunately, machines do malfunction. This means that the chances of scrap are not zero. The chances of scraping an entire batch of parts is, however, zero because we are not processing parts in batches. Should a part be scrapped, the operator will know it immediately as he or she tries to use the part in assembling the piece they are building. Problems, even major problems should be discovered after scraping only one part.

At this point, we know what we are trying to accomplish and we know what some of the major benefits should be. Exactly how do we design a factory around these ideas and principals?

To begin, we will start with a plan for material flow. Before we can determine material flow, we must decide what type of material will be used.

In Furniture Fabrication, there are two basic types of raw material that will feed the cell, sheet stock and wood components including wood panels. Each of these will be processed somewhat differently.

Sheet stock consists of sheets of material 4x8, 5x10 or other size. They can be MDF, particleboard, or wood core. They will generally have a decorative laminate or wood veneer on one or both faces.

In our new operation, these will be processed through, what is becoming known as "nested based manufacturing". That is, the entire sheet will be placed on the machine table. The parts, which have been nested on the sheet during the programming process, are cut into components ready to assemble. Material yield in this type of manufacturing can be quite high by industry standards.

The hardwood components or panels will be processed, generally using some type of conventional vacuum or clamp fixture to hold the parts. Whether you are using nested based manufacturing or wood component manufacturing, there is one key concept that must be understood, the material kit.

In traditional wood products manufacturing, materials are grouped and moved by size. For example, all the left sides of a chest are cut at the same time and a batch of these are stacked on a skid and moved from machine to machine and then to the final assembly area. The same is true of the right side and the back and all other components of the final product.

In Furniture Fabrication, however, material is grouped and handled in "material kits". A material kit includes all the material required to machine every component of the final product. One material kit equals one finished product.

This means that the sorting of material occurs at the rough mill or dimension plant, not at final assembly. The material is grouped into these material kits before it is sent to the furniture fabrication plant.

This idea of material kits is extremely important to the flow and operation of the Furniture Fabrication Factory. It is a different approach than most wood factories operate under today, but this simple change is key to the efficiencies possible with this new concept. If you want to build a single piece of furniture you simply retrieve a single material kit. If you want to build ten pieces you get ten kits and if you want to build a hundred you get a hundred kits.

With traditional material grouping, if you want to build just one piece of furniture, you might need to get twenty or thirty skids of material. Obviously this makes building one of anything virtually impossible from a cost standpoint. Costs are also very high for very small batches.

With traditional material grouping, there is a major cost penalty anytime the production batch size is different than the number of parts on a skid of material. Since each part can be a different size, a different number of them fit on a skid. A perfect balance is generally not possible. Maintaining proper material flow in this circumstance can become quite complex.

In traditional manufacturing, as soon as you run out of one component, the production run is over. It is common at that point to have extra parts on some, if not most of the skids. In theory, these parts can be stored and used the next time this piece is run. In practice, however, this seldom happens.

Generally, the parts are simply discarded. If you do take the time to remove and store the extra parts, you incur additional labor costs. Even then, you may not find them the next time you run the piece, or, they may have been knocked around enough that they are no longer usable.

Most of these problems disappear with the material kit. If the kits were sorted properly, there are no extra parts. In theory, when the production run is over, all the material has been used.

It is possible that a part is scrapped during the run. In this case, it is necessary to get a substitute from another kit. This will result in some extra parts, however, in traditional manufacturing these extra parts occur even without scrapping a part.

The area of handling scrapped parts during production will need some attention as companies begin to operate Furniture Fabrication Factories. It may be possible to cycle broken kits to a kit repair area where the missing parts are added and the kits returned to raw material. Since the kits are being returned directly to raw material inventory in exactly the same form as the original raw material, it is very likely that the material will be used in the future.

The really nice part of material kits is that the sorting occurs at the point that the material is first dimensioned. Extra pieces are much more likely to be reused or recycled at this point than if they occur at the final assembly point. The material is then handled in orderly bundles, which are quite easy to keep track of. It does not matter whether you plan to run one case or a hundred, the flow of material and the cost per case will be the same.

As you can see, material flow is quite simple. Material kits are brought into raw material and then moved to the proper cell when needed. Since production rates for a cell seldom result in more than a few complete pieces per cell per hour, the cell operator can be responsible for retrieving the needed material kits a couple times a day. Thus, it is important that the material kit storage be located as near as possible to the production cells.

For this reason, I am recommending a layout where a conveyor removes finished furniture from the center of the factory. Out from the central conveyor are the fabrication cells separated only by a short term holding area so that the finished pieces can be QC inspected before they move to the finishing room.

The next area out from the fabrication cells is an open material handling aisle and then material kit storage. The general layout is as follows:

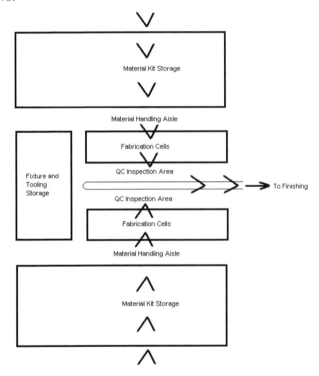

As you can see, this is a very simple, straightforward layout. Although this is not the only possible efficient layout, it is one that I feel will work very well after extensive testing of the various components. There are a lot of subtle aspects of this design that are not apparent when you first look at it.

You will notice, to the left of the fabrication cells is an area where the fixtures and tooling for the factory are stored. Not only is efficient handling for the material kits important, but efficient handling of the production fixtures is key to fast change over from producing one piece to the next.

This design is nice because, by extending it left to right, it is possible to vary the number of fabrication cells and thus the production capacity of the plant.

In the remainder of this book I will use this as a basic layout and offer a detailed view of how each of the key components of the system might work. The technology that I will describe already exists and has been tested unless I clearly state otherwise.

As this book is being written, this technology has not been used on a full scale factory operation. We do have a customer using furniture fabrication principals on a large scale but they are unwilling to allow us, or anyone else into their operations.

The efficient operation of this layout relies on several key capabilities and technology. It is these capabilities and technologies that we must focus on if we are to develop confidence that this system will work.

The three key aspects of this layout are; the smooth, easy flow of materials, the ability to perform every required machining and assembly function in the cell and the ability to change from producing one piece to producing a totally different piece very quickly.

Each of these areas is important and each can be quite involved. The next two chapters will address these fundamental requirements.

# Chapter 4

## Material Handling

# Chapter 4

## Material Handling

Just as we mentioned in the last chapter, the key to material flow in the Furniture Fabrication Factory is the material kit concept. If the primary material is sheet stock, sheets are simply stored and moved as a stack on a pallet. Any additional pieces needed are then bundled as a kit.

I believe that the best way to store material kits is on tall steel racks sorted by the furniture piece being built. There are a variety of rack storage systems available, and any of them will likely work, provided that a single operator is able to retrieve the material from the rack. From an operational standpoint, I believe that the machine operator should be able to retrieve his or her own material.

I have gotten some strange reactions when I suggested this. People believe that keeping the machine operating is so important that the machine operator should not stop to do anything else. A less qualified material handling person should do material handling. In theory, this is true. But like most theories, it doesn't quite work in practice.

In furniture fabrication, production batches will tend to be small. I believe that a production batch of one piece will be common. This means that once the piece is complete, material for the next piece must be available at the cell or production stops. In most factories, the material just won't be there.

When the cell operator completes the batch, he will need to find the material handling person and to get the next batch of material. This might take a couple of minutes, or it might take longer.

To eliminate the problem, perhaps material for the next batch or two could be retrieved and stored near the cell. This will eliminate the problem of running out of material, but it will cause another problem.

Now, the next couple of batches are fixed. The flexibility of being able to run anything next is gone. I believe that this flexibility will be important in the market of the future.

This practice will also cause congestion around the cell, reducing efficiency in addition to reducing flexibility. It also makes it much more difficult to keep track of material.

Instead of these approaches, I suggest that a method be found that allows the cell operator to retrieve the necessary material quickly. This is one of the reasons that I suggest storing the material kits on a tall rack storage system. Although these systems can become somewhat expensive, they do allow a lot of material to be stored in close proximity to the fabrication cells.

With a properly run material storage system, a cell operator can retrieve or replace material faster than he or she can find the material handler.

If the amount of raw material is kept to a minimum, it will not only reduce carrying costs, but it will also make locating and retrieving material easier. This means that an effective "just in time" supply line should be established.

I am a firm believer in safety margins, so I suggest that a few material kits for every current piece be maintained as a safety stock. With the furniture fabrication concept, this safety stock can actually give you the ability to produce anything in your current offering with zero notice. This is true flexibility.

Another area that must be addressed is material tracking. Every operator must be able to locate the exact material kit needed quickly and accurately. They must also be able to replace extra kits into inventory in such a way that the other operators can then find the kit.

It is also important that the exact status of the raw material inventory be instantly available to the material management or purchasing people.

Although there are several ways of accomplishing this material tracking requirement, the best way is by installing a series of networked PCs. These then operate an integrated inventory control software package. Each person that deals with the system can then use it to locate material. They also check out material used and input the new location for returned kits so that the system always knows exactly what is in inventory and where it is located.

This type of system offers access to the data to every cell operator. To operate properly, a certain level of discipline must be established. If the operators are properly motivated and if they understand the importance of an accurate database to their ability to do their job, the system will prove to be a valuable tool.

Furniture fabrication cells based on Thermwood's 91000 SuperControl can operate the inventory network right on the control itself. This eliminates the need for a separate PC at each fabrication cell.

The 91000 SuperControl is a full multi-tasking system. This means that it can execute more than one program at a time. Its major task is to operate the machine and this task has the highest priority. While it is operating the machine, however, it can also perform other tasks, such as communicating on a network. This offers a convenient method of communicating and solves one potentially serious problem.

That problem is that most PCs are not made to operate in the dusty environment of a furniture plant. Their operating life can be quite short in the factory. By using a multi-tasking machine control instead of a PC, you get the advantage of a sealed air-conditioned cabinet and a system that was specifically designed to operate in the dusty woodworking factory environment.

Many machine controls use a PC "front end" for their system to provide PC compatibility. It may be possible to use this PC to also communicate on the network. If not, a factory hardened PC may be needed at each cell.

In designing your material storage and retrieval system, make certain that you do not skimp on handling equipment, such as high-lift fork trucks or pallet trucks. If you decide to save some money by having a large number of cells use the same equipment, you will ultimately cost yourself a lot of money. Not only will conflicts arise as two or more cells require the equipment at the same time, but, a cell operator may have to travel a long distance to retrieve the equipment.

I would suggest that no more than two cells should share material handling equipment. This equipment will then sit idle most of the time. This is all right because, when a cell operator does need it, it will be waiting, readily available. Most cell operators will be able to retrieve material while their machine is actually running, provided that the retrieval process only takes a few minutes. The only way to provide this capability is to provide the equipment needed to retrieve materials available close by.

If you skimp on handling equipment, cell operators will need to wait for equipment at times. This will likely result in machine downtime. If this happens very often you will be paying for the material handling equipment over and over again in lost production.

In this analysis, I am assuming that the cell operator is motivated to produce as many good products as possible. This motivation will need to come from some type of production work or bonus program. This is an important area that we will cover in more detail later in this book.

The raw material inventory system will require a material handler to unload trucks and stage the material kits within the storage racks. This same handler should also be able to load out finished goods since he or she will not normally be needed for moving material within the factory. I see all material handling within the factory being accomplished by the cell operators themselves.

The final result is that a properly designed and equipped raw material storage system will support low raw material levels and a just-in-time delivery system, will assure that the correct materials are always available when needed and will do all this without special material handling people or without machine downtime.

So far in this chapter we have looked at raw material handling, but this is not the only material that must be handled. Unless you are operating strictly from sheet stock, special fixtures will be needed to hold the parts for machining. These fixtures will generally be the same size as the machine table. The most common size, I expect, will be four foot by eight foot.

A four foot by eight foot fixture is generally made of a ¾ inch thick piece of plywood, particleboard or MDF. This makes the fixture something that cannot be easily handled by one person.
To keep the flow going in the cell and to keep costs down, it is necessary to develop methods where one person can easily handle fixtures.

For this system to work properly, the cell operator must be able to change from one fixture to another and must be able to do this in, literally, a matter of a couple of minutes. To address this need, we have developed two new pieces of technology.

The first of these is the multi-function table that allows fixtures to be changed on the machine in a matter of a minute or less. Even though the fixture uses vacuum, there is no utility or vacuum hook up required. This even works for highly complex fixtures with multiple vacuum zones. We will cover this design and its operation in detail in Chapter 5- The Underlying Technology.

The second ingredient of the quick-change system is the fixture cart. This fixture cart allows one person to easily retrieve the new fixture from a fixture storage area, change fixtures at the machine and then store the old fixture.

In addition to the normal flat horizontal table, some Thermwood CNC routers are also equipped with vertical tables. These vertical tables are mounted to the left and right hand edges of the main table and extend down, toward the floor.

In operation, parts can be mounted to these vertical tables so that their edge is pointed upward. This allows normal vertical tooling to be used to perform edge work such as tenoning or dovetailing.

These vertical tables also require a spoilboard or fixture. The fixture cart is also used to remove and replace these vertical fixtures.

The main part of the fixture cart consists of two roller tables. Each table can hold a full sized spoilboard. It has free rollers covering the top surface so the spoilboard or fixture can be rolled on and off the table while lying in the horizontal plane. Ninety degrees to this table are a set of edge rollers. The entire table can be tipped up so that the fixture is standing on its edge, lying on the edge rollers. A guide along the top edge assures that the fixture doesn't simply fall away from the table.

The multi-function table, which we will explain in more detail in Chapter 5, has a retaining lip around the entire outer edge. The fixture or spoilboard is inserted into the cavity made by this edge. The edge of the table locates the fixture and system vacuum holds the fixture in place.

To change fixtures, move the fixture cart to the machine. The new fixture should be loaded onto one of the two cart tables and should be in the vertical position. The second cart table should be empty and placed in the horizontal position.

The next step is to remove the existing fixture. Turn off the system vacuum and lift the edge of the fixture. A pushpin located at the front edge of the table will assist you in lifting the front edge. Now simply pull the fixture off the machine and onto the fixture cart table.

Rotate that table to the vertical position. Next, rotate the table containing the new fixture to the horizontal position and pull the new fixture onto the machine table. Once the fixture is dropped into the table the system vacuum can be turned on and the fixture change is complete.

You might want to study the above photos so that you can understand the process completely. The change over is quite simple and only requires a couple of minutes.

Once the system vacuum is turned on, the fixture is held in place and the fixture vacuum system is energized. This supplies vacuum to the valves controlling vacuum to the various zones of the fixture. All of the technology surrounding this vacuum system will be discussed in detail in the technology chapter of this book.

Once the old fixture has been removed and the new fixture loaded, the fixture cart, with the old fixture, is rolled to the fixture storage rack. This rack is designed to store fixtures on edge in the vertical position. The cart is simply rolled to the storage rack and The fixture pushed off the cart and into the rack.

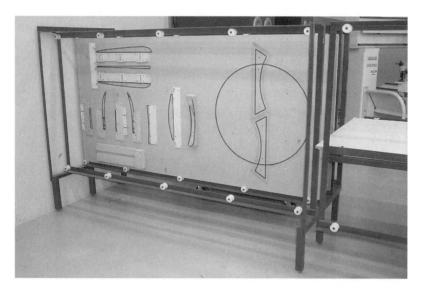

The fixture cart has an additional set of rollers under the table which are used to store and move vertical table fixtures. Fixtures for the vertical table are smaller and lighter than the full table fixtures and can simply be removed by hand and slid into the fixture cart. The new fixture is rolled out of the cart and placed on the machine.

This fixture change process actually takes longer to describe that to actually do. By incorporating the fixture cart and fixture storage rack with the multi-function table, a complete system for rapidly changing fixtures is available. The system has the added advantage that a fixture can be retrieved, changed and the old fixture replaced by a single operator. This fixture change system is key to the fast changeover required for furniture fabrication.

The final area we will discuss in this material handling area is the removal of the finished article of furniture from the fabrication cell.

Again, we will want this to happen without the need for special material handling people to actually move the material. The concept I am going to present is quite simple. It will provide an aid to the assembly process, will provide an easy way to move the final product away from the fabrication cell and will also provide a means to move the product through the finishing room.

The key ingredient of this system is a material-handling cart. This cart rolls on the floor on casters. It has a flat top on which the piece of furniture bring processed can be assembled. Once assembly and sanding is complete, the cart is moved away from the fabrication cell.

The next step in the process depends on the specific procedures in place concerning quality control. If a special quality control inspector must inspect and approve the piece before finishing, the cart is rolled to an inspection area and left. Otherwise, it is moved to an in-floor moving conveyor drive that moves past each of the fabrication cells. The assembly cart is then clipped to this conveyor drive. The cart is then pulled to, and through, the finishing operation.

If the piece must be inspected first, the QC inspector is then responsible for attaching the cart to the drive once the piece has been approved for finishing. Otherwise, the cell operator is the one who attaches the cart to the conveyor that carries it away.

There are some subtle additions to this system that will make it even nicer. A simple cardholder can be attached to the cart. The cell operator places a preprinted production card in this holder. This production card carries all of the information required for manufacturing, assembly and finishing. This data may very well be in the form of bar codes.

I believe that in the future you will be required to either custom build, or at least offer production variations for individual customers. A customer may be able to not only select the piece of furniture but may also be able to select the finish, hardware and maybe even profile shapes or designs on the piece.

This cart system with the production card makes handling these variations simple. Information and bar codes that define all the variables needed for the piece are printed on the card. It may even contain the individual customer name for this piece.

During the fabrication process, the card becomes the guide to input necessary variables into the fabrication program. As the piece moves to finishing, the card defines the finish that should be used. It then defines the final hardware, packaging and perhaps shipping address.

This concept involves several pieces of technology that most woodworkers are not familiar with. I would like to talk about some of these starting with the actual machining of the parts.

It is possible today, to use a single program to make an almost unlimited variety of parts. This is generally called parametric programming. The concept behind parametric programming is quite simple, but the final result is very powerful.

To understand parametric programming, let us use a very simple example. In this example we will make a door that has a hardware hole drilled directly in the center. Let us imagine that the door is 12 inches wide by 18 inches long.

To program this door, we will first cut the outside perimeter. Starting from the upper left corner, we cut 12 inches in one direction across the top of the door. We then cut 18 inches along the right side, 12 inches back across the bottom and 18 inches up the left side. We have now machined the outside of the door. We now move 6 inches across the top and 9 inches down. This puts us directly in the center of the door where we can drill the center hole.

As programs go, this one is quite simple but should work very well. It will make 12 inch by 18 inch doors all day long. But, what if we want a 10 inch by 20 inch door? Normally, you need to create another program that makes a 10 by 20 inch door. This is not too difficult to do, but what if every door is a different size. Do we need to create a new program for every door?

This is where parametric programming comes in. In parametric programming, the program is created, not with exact dimensions but with variables instead. These variables are then defined just before the program is run. To better understand this, let us go back to our door example.

For this program we will define two variables. We will call the width of the door *width*, and we will call the length of the door *length*. We will now write the same program using the variables *width* and *length* instead of the actual door size.

Starting in the upper left corner, we move across the top, a distance called *width*. We then move down the right side a distance called *length*. We move across the bottom a distance called *width* and up the left side a distance called *length*.

As you can see, if we substitute 12 inches for *width* and 18 inches for *length*, this program will cut a 12 by 18 inch door, just like our original program. If we want a 10 by 20 inch door, however, we don't need a new program. We simply define *width* as 10 inches and *length* as 20 inches and the same program now makes a 10 by 20 inch door.

In fact, you can assign any size to *width* and *length* and cut the outside of any size door using the same program. As you can see, this is an extremely powerful capability, but we have only scratched the surface.

Let us go back to our door and see how we handle the hardware hole in the center. This time, instead of moving a fixed distance to the center of the door, we will move *width* divided by 2 (*width*/2) and *length* divided by 2 (*length*/2). On the 12 by 18 inch door, we will move 12 divided by 2 or 6 inches on one axis and 18 divided by 2 or 9 inches on the other axis. This is the same distance we moved on our first program. In fact, these simple formulas will always move to the center of the door, regardless of the values assigned to *width* and *length*.

This is an extremely simple example. The real power lies in the fact that virtually any mathematical function can be performed in the program including complex trigonometric functions. A single program can be used to produce a variety of different sizes and different designs.

Certain variables can even define which design is to be cut. For example, we could define a variable called *design*. We could then use logical commands to determine which design to run. For example, if we define *design* as 1, we could drill the hardware hole in the center as we have been doing. If we define *design* as 2, we could drill the hole near the top of the door, using a different set of program commands and if we define *design* as 3 we could drill the hole near the bottom of the door.

When the program is run, the control determines the value of the variable *design* and then executes the program commands associated with that value. By simply changing the value of a variable, you can change the design of the part being produced.

As you can see, parametric programming offers tremendous possibilities for customizing products in an efficient production environment. When I talk to furniture makers about customizing their end products, I generally get a highly negative reaction indicating that this is totally impossible in their industry. As you can see by these simple examples, it is not only possible but is actually rather easy to do.

In the first chapter I discussed the problems the industry is facing and will face with low cost foreign labor. The single biggest problem that goods produced outside the US has is the fact that product must be shipped long distances to reach the final customer. Even if the cost is not significant, this takes time.

If the US furniture industry could convince the market that it needs high quality furniture customized just for them, we could gain a major competitive advantage. We could produce this "semi-custom" furniture at a low cost and deliver it to the customer very quickly. Even if the foreign competition could figure out how to customize, they would still be faced with substantial obstacles in keeping track of and delivering furniture in the short time frame the market will demand. In this type of market, the U.S. furniture industry would have a fundamental competitive advantage.

As I continue through this book, I will continue to focus on the idea of knowing the customer before you produce the product even though I know that this is not how things work today. I will continue in this direction because this may very well be one of the few ways we can keep the furniture industry in the U.S.

Parametric programs are not a new concept. Most parametric programs however, are handled within a software package such as a CAD/CAM package. This software actually generates part programs. In this software, the variables are assigned and a program generated, usually automatically, that produces a part based on the value of the variables. The control system then executes this program just like any other program because it is just like any other program.

This approach can actually function in a furniture fabrication cell, but its operation would require a programmer that develops the necessary programs and downloads these to each of the controls as they are needed. With certain types of production using a nested manufacturing, this approach will result in a significant material yield improvement. Using this approach, the fabrication cell might never run the same program twice, even if it is producing the exact same piece of furniture. These program variations are necessary to make the best possible use of the sheet material.

This is quite a change from current practices where the programs are fixed and material yield is determined by the program itself. Under this new approach, perhaps a dresser, chest and two nightstands are produced in a batch. The parts for all three pieces may be nested together on various sheets to obtain the best material yield. In fact, the first sheet used might only be a partial sheet left over from the last batch.

This technology is currently being used in the cabinet industry in essentially the way I have described it. This same technology can also be applied to the manufacture of furniture and this technology is essential to manufacturing mass customized furniture.

For straight parametric programs, Thermwood has developed what, I believe is a ideal way of addressing this situation.

Thermwood's SuperControl handles parametric programs within the control itself using a feature called the Advanced Function Language. In addition to the ability to execute the standard EIA program code, the SuperControl can also interpret and execute a series of programming commands within the program. Using the Advanced Function Language, it is possible to write programs using variables instead of fixed numbers. Methods are available to define the value for these variables before a program is run. The program will then execute with those assigned values.

The Advanced Function Language also allows mathematical and logical functions to be performed using both variables and fixed numbers.

The final result is that complex parametric programs can be used, right at the control and the variables can be defined by simply scanning a bar code. This means that the final design of the furniture piece can be defined at the order entry point and then coded on a production card. The production card is then scanned at the fabrication cell to define the variables for this particular piece of furniture.

The Advanced Function Language is not restricted to just parametric programming. It has many other advanced capabilities that are important to this new manufacturing method. We will discuss some of these advanced capabilities in the technology chapter of this book.

At this point, however, you can see the importance of the production card that is carried on the material-handling cart.

In addition to providing design data to the fabrication cell, the production card also provides finishing data to the finishing room.

Just as I expect that the actual design of furniture will allow for a certain level of customization through parametric programming, I also believe that each piece will be offered in a variety of finishes. The production card will define the finish that must be placed on the piece.

While I do not intend to explore the finishing room in detail, there are a few points that are important enough to address. The most important point is that the finishing room must have the ability to spray any finish available at random without the need for clean up or color changeover.

There are several way of doing this and this concept is not all that new. The most straightforward way is to equip each spray booth with a separate material delivery system for each different material or color. There is some cost involved in doing this, however, it is necessary to allow the random application of whatever finish is required for each piece.

You may not need a separate system for every final result. It is possible to combine different features to obtain a large variety of end products with a few variations at each station. For example, you could use five different stains from very light to very dark. That gives you five different variations. You could then add a distressing gun so each color is now available either distressed or not. You now have ten variations. You could then add three different levels of gloss in the overcoat. You now have thirty finish variations.

I think you get the idea. The actual variations must be worked out at each factory. This opens up a whole new area for material and technical development. But you can see, in this example you require five stain guns, one distressing gun and three overcoat guns to apply thirty different finishes.

I have actually seen this approach, using multiple guns, used in furniture finishing rooms. The only possible drawback is that the spray operator must determine exactly which spray gun to use. The necessary information can be carried on the production card, however, this information must be interpreted and then properly executed by the operator. Any process that requires human interpretation is prone to error. Due care must be exercised to make certain that these errors are kept to a minimum.

Although I have not kept up with spray technology, I have seen systems within the auto industry where a single system could deliver a multitude of material colors, changing from one to another almost instantly. The ideal solution would be this type of system, which could respond to bar code input. The bar code on the production card could then be used to automatically select the proper material without the chance for interpretation errors.

There are some other areas that must be considered in this type of operation. When you are finishing a batch of product to the same finish schedule, it is relatively easy to keep the color and application uniform between pieces. This is important when several pieces will sold as a suite for use in a single customer room. The pieces must have a finish that matches relatively well.

When you are spraying a variety of finishes at random, the problem of achieving uniformity is more difficult. This area must be addressed. One method that can work is to provide a match plate at each finishing station for each finish. A sample piece of material is available to the finish operator to show how the piece should look as it exits that station. While this sounds crude, it actually works relatively well provided your material supplier provides consistent finishing materials.

Another important point to consider is that you cannot take shortcuts in equipment selection. The best possible agitation tanks, handling and delivery equipment are necessary to assure consistency. Any additional costs involved will be returned a hundred fold by eliminating problem variations in finishing.

The handling cart concept provides some real flexibility in the finishing room. Again, the most straightforward approach is to simply have the conveyor pull the carts through the finishing room. It can move through the spray booths, past the wiping areas and through the ovens all the way to final packing.

In smaller operations, however, there are some simpler alternatives. The material handling carts can be simply unhooked from the conveyor and rolled by hand to the various stations. Air drying becomes an option. In a relatively small operation, only a few pieces per hour may be built, a couple of people may be able to handle all the finishing operations. As the operation grows, more people are added and eventually a full scale automatic operation can evolve.

One of the advantages of furniture fabrication is that the same concept works well for both small and large scale operations. It is possible to efficiently build furniture with a single fabrication cell, a single spray booth and a few employees. The overall investment in this operation will be substantially less than what would be required to build furniture in the more traditional fashion. Today, to operate a furniture factory there is a certain minimum volume requirement and minimum investment requirement. Furniture fabrication dramatically lowers those minimum numbers while building a price competitive product.

As this book is being written we have already had a three man cabinet shop begin making bedroom furniture using this technology. Before these technical developments, I do not believe that there was any way this could have happened. Today, the barriers to starting the manufacture of furniture have collapsed. It no longer requires a multitude of machines and decades of experience.

In this chapter we have discussed some of the material flow and material handling concepts for furniture fabrication. In the next chapter we will explore some of the new technology that make furniture fabrication possible.

# Chapter 5

## The Underlying Technology

# Chapter 5

## The Underlying Technology

At this point you should be starting to get the flavor of how this new factory might work. If you work in the industry, you have also thought of many problems and stumbling blocks that could prevent this from working as it really should.

In this chapter we are going to explore these stumbling blocks. A large body of new technology already exists that addresses many of these potential problem areas. The furniture industry, however, is generally not aware of the existence of much of this technology. In this chapter we will explore this technology and discuss the practical aspects of its use.

We have already mentioned the multi-function machine table several times, so, let us begin by looking at it in more detail.

For many years, CNC routers used a slab type table. This consisted of essentially a sheet of material such as plywood, aluminum or composite material. Some companies built a steel or aluminum frame and then covered this frame with the sheet of material. This slab table was then either drilled for hold down bolts or equipped with clamps to hold a fixture or spoilboard.

While this approach is rather simple and straightforward, it did require that the fixture be manually located and mechanically fastened to the tabletop. This added time to the changeover process from one part to the next. The multi-function table was the result of a desire to change from one fixture to the next using a minimum of time. This is accomplished by fundamentally changing the way that conventional vacuum is used on the machine.

There are essentially two types of vacuum used to hold parts, conventional vacuum and Universal Vacuum. Conventional vacuum is typically used to hold smaller parts and hardwood panels. Universal Vacuum is used to hold relatively flat sheet stock and larger flat parts. Furniture fabrication will use either or both systems depending on the type of material being processed.

Conventional vacuum typically uses a fixture equipped with a soft rubber seal that runs around the edge of the part. Vacuum at about 10 PSI is ported to the center of the seal area and the vacuum holds the part to the fixture for machining. Some type of vacuum plenum was commonly used to port vacuum to the appropriate place inside the seal area.

A vacuum plenum was also used in the second type of vacuum hold down, Universal Vacuum. Universal Vacuum is a system developed by Thermwood in the mid 80's to hold panels to the spoilboard without the need for special fixtures and vacuum seals.

Universal Vacuum consists of a high flow vacuum source connected to a hollow plenum that is covered with a porous spoilboard. The spoilboard is commonly made of certain types of MDF or particleboard. Vacuum under the spoilboard pulls air continuously through the spoilboard. Any part laid on this tabletop is then held in place by this airflow.

Although the system sounds like magic, it works quite well for flat panel stock and is in widespread use today. A variation being used today in nested-based manufacturing uses a thin handling sheet that is also porous. A pegboard that has been sanded smooth works quite well as a handling sheet.

The purpose of the handling sheet is to aid in removing the nest of parts from the tabletop after it has been cut. The sheet material to be cut is laid on top of the handling sheet and both are moved onto the machine table. Universal Vacuum holds the sheet material firmly in place, right through the handling sheet.

The material is machined cutting all the way through the base material, but not through the handling sheet. It is possible to cut all the way through the material and only cut slightly into the handling sheet.

When the cycle is complete, a number of nested parts have been cut from the sheet of material. To unload the machine, the handling sheet, which is still fully in tact, is simply pulled off the table with all the nested parts still in place. A new sheet is loaded and cutting continues while the previously cut parts are labeled and sorted. Once all the parts have been removed, the handling sheet can be reused.

This process is simple, straightforward and highly efficient. It results in high machine utilization while supporting the manufacture of random part designs.

The multi-function table combines the ability to use both conventional vacuum and Universal Vacuum on a single table. It also provides a system where the spoilboard or vacuum fixture can be changed quickly, without the need for mechanical clamps or screws to hold the fixture in place. It also does not require that vacuum valves be disconnected or connected when fixtures are changed.

The multi-function table consists of a tooled aluminum table that has a built in vacuum plenum. It also has a locating lip all the way around the perimeter of the table. The fixture or spoilboard is sized so that it fits snugly into the table inside the locating lip. A vacuum seal goes all the way around the edge of the table, approximately an inch inside the lip. This vacuum seal effectively seals the fixture or spoilboard to the table when the vacuum is turned on.

If you load the fixture and turn on vacuum, the fixture will seal against the table and will be held rigidly in place. On a five foot by five foot table running conventional vacuum the fixture is held in place by about 36,000 pounds of force. On a five by ten table this becomes 72,000 pounds. This provides a highly rigid table and fixture assembly.

On typical CNC router tables the main machine vacuum is used to turn vacuum on and off to hold the part in place. If there are two or more vacuum zones, there needs to be two or more main vacuum valves.

On the multi-function table, main vacuum is used to hold the fixture to the table. It is turned on when the new fixture is put in place and then left on. One or more tabletop valves, mounted to the fixture itself, are then used to turn vacuum on and off for each vacuum zone in order to hold the parts in place.

Although this arrangement is somewhat difficult to explain, it is actually quite easy to set up and use. Instead of simply porting vacuum from under the fixture to the seal area, it is ported outside the seal area to a table-mounted valve. Vacuum from this valve is then ported inside the seal area so that the table mounted valve controls the vacuum that holds the part.

To understand this better, refer to the following drawing.

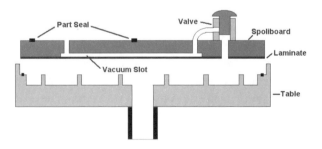

As you can see, when the fixture is set into the table and vacuum is turned on, the vacuum will hold the fixture in place. In addition, it will feed vacuum to the vacuum control valve.

When the vacuum valve is pulled to the up, open position, vacuum is channeled through the bottom slot to the area inside the part seal.

This has the advantage that a fixture can be equipped with as many zones as necessary and each fixture can be equipped with a different number of vacuum zones. Regardless of the number of zones, all that is necessary to install the fixture is to drop it in place and turn on the main vacuum.

This provides a simple system that is highly effective and highly flexible. From this simple building block, complex vacuum fixtures can be built.

The first thing you will discover as you try and design fixtures for furniture fabrication is that seldom can you fit all the parts for a piece of furniture on the table at one time. This is especially true when trying to build furniture from wood components and panels rather than sheet stock. This means that some areas of the table may need to be shared by several parts. Generally these parts will not be the same size, so a method is needed that holds different sized parts using conventional vacuum and seals.

When tooling several complex pieces for trade shows, we have developed an effective technique and I believe that this method will work well for almost any kind of furniture fabrication. This technique uses multiple hold down areas that are controlled by a single vacuum valve. Each zone of the table is made up of several areas and can hold several different sized panels.

The zone is segmented into several independent sealed areas. When a part is laid in the zone, it covers certain areas but not others. The areas that are not covered are sealed using rubber stoppers.

The trick to designing these zones is to locate the sealed areas so that every panel size assigned to the zone completely covers certain areas while totally avoiding all other areas. In this way, the panel perimeter can be trimmed without cutting through a seal.

To understand this concept better, let us develop a simple example. We will start with three different panel sizes as shown below.

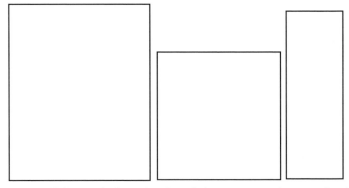

Because of the variations in size, it is apparent that no single seal can adequately hold all three parts. To create seal areas within the zone, we will lay all three parts on top of each other with the right bottom corner of each part at the same location. We will use that right bottom corner to locate the panels within the zone by using a fence or locator pins. The three panels will then look like this:

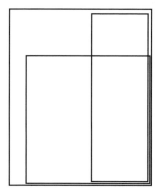

At this point, it is quite clear that there are four separate vacuum areas. A seal can now be cut inside each of these areas like this:

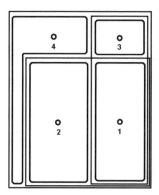

We now have one vacuum zone that can hold four different sized parts using conventional vacuum. The vacuum ports, numbered 1, 2, 3 and 4 are drilled from the top surface into channels cut under the fixture. A vacuum valve controls vacuum to this channel.

In order to configure the zone for the different sized panels, rubber stoppers are used in the ports that are not covered by the part. For example, consider the following part;

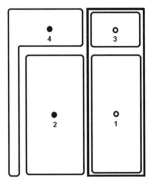

In this example, the part covers areas 1 and 3. Stoppers are placed in ports 2 and 4 to seal vacuum in those areas. When the vacuum valve is activated, the resulting vacuum holds the part through areas 1 and 3. The perimeter of the part does not cross any vacuum seal so a router bit can pass completely through the part all the way around the part perimeter. Now let's switch to another sized panel.

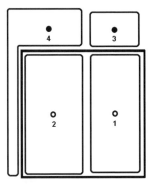

In this example, the part covers areas 1 and 2. Ports 3 and 4 are plugged using the rubber stoppers. Again, you can see that the entire perimeter can be trimmed without cutting through a vacuum seal.

The third part covers all four areas of this vacuum zone.

Thus you can see that one vacuum zone on the table can be used to hold several different sized parts by creating vacuum seal areas.

Most furniture will require several zones at different locations on the table, each zone is controlled by a separate valve and includes several hold down areas. If you attempt to accommodate too many different sizes in one zone, too many small vacuum areas result. The holding areas inside the seals become small and changing rubber stoppers becomes tedious.

The rubber stoppers are designed so that they protrude far enough above the tabletop so that if you attempt to lay a part over a stopper, the part will hit the stopper and will not lie on the vacuum seal. It is quite easy to realize that a port stopper has not been properly removed. It is not possible to seal and hold a part with the stopper in place.

Once a part has been laid in place, any port that you can see without a stopper must be plugged. It helps to paint the inside of each port red. This red color is covered up when the stopper is in place. It is quite easy to spot an open port if it is painted red.

For many products, an audio file plays instructions to the operator during the cycle. Some cycles are quite long and complex and the audio files seem to offer the quickest and easiest way of providing information to the operator about the order in which parts are to run. The audio file also tells the operator which zone the next part will use and which areas within the zone to open.

By calling different files at different places in the program, you can effectively provide the operator with the necessary instructions.

There is some unique technology around playing the audio files, which we will cover later in this chapter

There are several methods of locating a part at each zone. A fence can be installed at the reference corner for each zone, however, it is necessary to use a corner spacer if the perimeter of the panel will be trimmed. This spacer is normally an aluminum "L" about three quarters of an inch thick. It is first laid into the locator fence and then the part is pushed against the spacer. Vacuum is turned on to hold the part and then the spacer is removed, leaving the part properly located but spaced away from the locator fence. Its edge is now exposed and can be trimmed all the way around without the bit hitting the fence.

Thermwood sells an aluminum locator fence that uses spring-loaded pins to locate the spacer. This offers an advantage over the simpler fixed fence.

With a fixed fence, once the part has been secured by vacuum, the spacer may be tightly wedged between the fixed fence and the part. Sometimes it is difficult to remove the spacer, since it must be pulled straight up evenly.

With a pin locator, once the part has been secured, the pin retracts and it is easy to simply roll the spacer out of the fence.

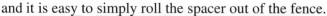

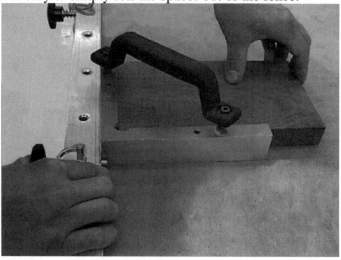

Most of the major part hold down techniques will be used at one point or another in fixturing for furniture fabrication. All of the fixtures and part hold down zones, however, are mounted on a single fixture board. This board can then be simply lifted out of the table lip and quickly replaced. The ability to quickly replace a fixture does have one possible drawback. Since it is so easy to replace an entire part fixture, less care may be taken in identifying the fixture and program.

In most instances in furniture fabrication, the operator will actually accomplish the fixture change. It is apparent that some method of assuring that the correct fixture is matched with the correct part program is needed. We call this system automatic fixture verification.

The basic idea is very simple. A permanent bar code is affixed to the fixture. A special code is added to the beginning of the part program. This code includes the fixture identification number for the correct fixture for this program.

When the program is run for the first time, the control will stop and instruct the operator to scan the bar code on the fixture. If the number on the fixture matches the fixture number in the program, program execution continues. If the number does not match, the system informs the operator that the fixture is incorrect.

This fixture check only occurs the first time a newly loaded program is run. Once the fixture number checks out, the program can be run over and over again without the need to check the fixture again. As soon as a new program is loaded, the new fixture must be checked against the new program.

This simple fixture verification can avoid costly errors that might otherwise occur.

Fixture verification relies on a common technology that is not readily available on CNC controls, bar code input. In furniture fabrication, bar code capability is essential. It allows new programs to be selected and loaded with a simple scan. It virtually eliminates typing input errors and allows cell operators that are not proficient at working with a computer to operate the fabrication cell. For furniture fabrication, make certain that the control you use can accept bar code input.

The bar code system Thermwood uses utilizes printed bar codes that simply replace keystrokes from the keyboard. This means that virtually any input or selection you can make through the keyboard can also be made using a printed bar code.

Once the new program has been loaded and the proper fixture installed and verified, there is still one additional area that must be addressed, tooling.

It is very unlikely that the tools currently in the machine are the correct tools for the new part. It is likely that some, or all of the tools will need to be changed.

In the past, changing tools has been a skilled job requiring a certain level of knowledge, judgement and skill. Unfortunately, every cell operator may not possess the required level of knowledge, judgement and skill. In fact, even experienced setup people make tooling errors.

Once again, modern technology is coming to the rescue in the form of automatic tool management, but before we talk about automatic tool management, we need to explore the world of automatic tool changers.

Automatic tool changers rely on a specially designed tooling spindle. This spindle uses a drawbar to pull a tapered tool holder into a tapered receptacle at the bottom of the spindle. This drawbar has several fingers that grip a knob screwed into the end of the tool holder. When the drawbar retracts, it pulls the tool holder tightly into the spindle taper. The drawbar is pulled upward by a series of strong springs located at the top of the spindle.

To change tools, the spindle is stopped and a hydraulic or multi-stage pneumatic cylinder pushes down on the drawbar. This collapses the retaining springs and pushes the tool holder away from the spindle taper. At this point, the tool holder can be snapped out of the drawbar by simply pulling down on it.

This tool change spindle is common to all automatic tool changers. At this point, however, there are a large variety of methods for removing the old tool holder and inserting a new one.

All the various tool change systems, however, can be divided into two categories. In the first category the spindle travels to the changer to change tools and in the second category the tool changer travels with the head.

The simplest, and least expensive, form of tool changer is the bar style. A series of snap in tool holders are located at the rear of the machine table. To change tools, the head moves to an empty holder and deposits the current tool. It then moves to the location of the next tool and retrieves it. All movements use the X and Y axes of the machine and there are no separate moving parts in the tool changer other than the spindle itself.

Obviously this system is both simple and inexpensive when compared to other systems. It is also quite reliable since it doesn't have any moving parts. It does, however have a couple of limitations.

The most obvious shortcoming is that the head may need to move quite a distance to the location where the tools are stored. This was a major drawback in the past, however, new CNC routers are so fast that the extra time required is not nearly as significant as it once was. The second drawback is that, because of head clearance, a limited number of tools can be mounted on the back of the table.

Thermwood has addressed this limited availability problem by developing the bulk tool changer. This system sits to the side of the machine and has a single load/unload station. The tools are carried on a large chain driven by a servomotor.

To change tools using a bulk tool changer, the head moves to the load/unload position and deposits the existing tool. The chain then rapidly positions the next tool, which is retrieved by the head.

The bulk tool changer can hold up to fifty tools. One machine can be equipped with two bulk tool changers for a total of one hundred tools. Generally, one bulk tool changer is sufficient to hold enough tools to produce every part that might be processed by a furniture fabrication cell.

Just like the bar tool changer, however, the bulk tool changer does require that the head move to the tool changer, which takes time. This brings up the second type of automatic tool changer, the one that travels with the head.

An automatic tool changer that travels with the head can change tools essentially anywhere on the table. Thus, the head does not need to travel to a specific position to retrieve the new tool. This should mean quicker tool changes, but until recently, it has also meant a complex mechanism.

"At the head" automatic tool changers have required one, two sometimes three degrees of freedom in the mechanism to change tools. This means that the tools must slide and rotate, or slide and flip, or slide and rotate and flip. The design made the devices more difficult to maintain and adjust as well as making them more expensive.

Despite the limitations, however, they did provide faster tool changes.

Recently, Thermwood developed a single degree of freedom at-the-head automatic tool changer called the "typewriter" tool changer. It is called the "typewriter" tool changer because it operates very much like the old manual typewriters.

On an old typewriter, when you pressed a key, an arm would move to a spot and type a letter. When you pressed another key, another arm would move to the same spot and type a different letter. In fact, every key you pressed would send another arm to the same spot to type its letter.

The typewriter tool changer works the same way. Five different tools are loaded on five different arms. Each arm can swing the tool to the same spot under the spindle. To change tools, an arm with an empty holder is swung under the spindle and the current tool is replaced. That arm swings the tool out of the way and another arm with the new tool swings it into position. The new tool is retrieved and the tool change is complete.

This system has several advantages. First, it is simple so it should be quite reliable. Also, by being simple it is also lower cost than other at-the-head tool changers. Finally, it is fast. Swinging the arm in and out can happen quickly. Just think how fast a manual typewriter works.

As with any at-the-head tool changer, it has the disadvantage that it carries a limited number of tools. Thus, it shares the disadvantage with all at-the-head automatic tool changers that the correct tools must be loaded into the correct holders each time a new program is loaded. Again, knowledge, judgement and skill are needed. And again, technology comes to the rescue.

A system called automatic tool management combines the typewriter tool changer with the bulk tool changer. Thus, it overcomes most of the limitations and shortcomings of the more traditional approach.

First, certain tools are too large in diameter to fit the typewriter tool changer. These tools remain in the bulk tool changer and if they are needed during a cycle, the head moves to the bulk tool changer and retrieves it. The real advantage of the system, however, is that the bulk tool changer and the typewriter tool changer interact automatically to manage those tools that will fit in the typewriter tool changer.

To understand how this works, let us assume that the operator has loaded a new program. When the start button is pressed the first time, the system will first determine which tools the program will need. It will take the tools currently in the typewriter tool changer and will place them back in the bulk tool changer. It will then automatically retrieve from the bulk tool changer the tools needed for the new program.

If the program requires more tools than the typewriter tool changer can hold, the system will retrieve those tools that will result in the best overall cycle time. During program execution, the remainder of the tools will be retrieved directly from the bulk tool changer.

The significant part of this technology is that all this occurs automatically, without any real input from the operator. Again, errors can be virtually eliminated and less technically skilled people can function as cell operators.

Another type of automatic tool changer is not a tool changer in the traditional sense. It is the rotary turret. This is a large eight position rotating head. Each of the eight positions can be equipped with a different head. The advantage of the rotary turret is that it supports essentially different heads.

A turret can be equipped with vertical routers, horizontal routers, shapers, planers, saws, vertical drills and horizontal drills. This offers a high level of flexibility and, rotary turrets change from one tool to the next very quickly.

The only real downside to the rotary turret is that you are limited to eight tools and tool change is a manual task.

The key requirements for changing from producing one piece of furniture to another are; selecting and loading the correct program, changing the fixture if necessary and loading the proper tools in the proper tool locations. As you have just seen, this entire process has been virtually automated.

The correct program can be located, selected and loaded by simply scanning a bar code on a work order. Instructions at the beginning of the program can identify the correct fixture to load. The correct fixture can be simply slipped into position and the system will make certain that the correct fixture was installed. It won't run with the wrong fixture. The system will also automatically retrieve the correct tools and place them in the correct locations. Add the material kit which has the correct raw materials sorted by finished product and there is very little that can go wrong compared to how things operate today.

Each part of the technology I have just described exists and is being shipped today. These are not pie-in-the-sky ideas, but is instead an overall integrated system that really works in the real, everyday world. As with many new technical areas, much of what I have just described is covered by patents or pending patents. Before you put these ideas into operation make certain that you have the legal right to use them.

While we are talking about tooling, there are several other areas that we should discuss.

The first of these has to do with tool life. When we ran thousands of parts at a time, it was relatively easy to keep track of tool life. You knew that a certain tool would run three hours or six hours, or perhaps a certain number of board feet. You could pretty well guess about when the tool needed to be changed. A good manager would change the tool before it began making scrap.

Now the world is changed. A tool may be picked up and used to make five or ten parts and then it may not be used again for days. Some tools are used a lot and others may only be used a few times a month. This makes it very difficult to keep track of when to change tools. To make matters worse, you might need to keep track of fifty to a hundred tools per machine.

The truth is that you cannot keep track of tools manually. Without a system to track tool usage, the only way you will know that a tool needs to be changed is when it begins making bad parts. That is just too late.

Fortunately, there are sophisticated tool management systems that solve this problem. Thermwood's SuperControl has a complete tool management system and other CNC controls may have similar capabilities. In the remainder of the discussion on tool management I will use Thermwood's system capability as the basis. If you intend to use another system for furniture fabrication you will need to determine the tool management capability of that system.

Tool management in the Thermwood machine works through a series of fill-in-the-blank tables that contain all the basic information concerning the tool, spindle, changers, etc. Each tool is assigned a number and the program calls the tool by the tool number.

One of the fields in the tool management screen is the life remaining box. This field contains the number of hours of actual cutting that you expect from the tool. As the tool is used, the actual cutting time is subtracted from the current remaining life. When the remaining life reaches zero, a message is displayed at the bottom of the screen. Once this message appears, it is time to change tools.

The actual life needs to be determined by trial and error. After a specific tool has been used several times, the life you can reasonably expect will become apparent. It is important to set the life so that it expires before you begin to run scrap parts. In furniture fabrication, with its use of material kits, scrap parts have a much larger impact than in traditional manufacturing. This is a major reason why a system to track tool use and alert the operator just before a tool becomes unusable is important.

Thermwood's tool management system has one additional feature. In each tool table you can specify a different tool to use if the current tool life has expired. If you have a tool that is used extensively, you may have several of these installed in the system at one time. When the first one wears out, the system automatically replaces it with the next one. This allows much more time for the tooling manager to service the machines.

Another aspect of tool management is the requirement that the tool length be set. This can be accomplished in several ways. The first, but most difficult is to try and set the length of the tool accurately within the tool holder. If the program was written for a tool that extends two inches from the tool holder, then you attempt to position all replacement tools exactly two inches out. This is easier said than done.

The first problem is that tool holders are not all exactly the same dimensions. If you reference the face of the tool holder, the actual position of the tip of the tool may not be in exactly the same place if different tool holders are used. It is possible to use a special fixture that references the clamp ring on the tool holder. This will generally result in better tolerances, however, even the taper can vary slightly from one tool holder to another resulting in variations in the length of the tool.

A better way is to actually insert the tool in the spindle and then measure the length of the tool and place this value in a tool table. For machines that allow for tool length compensation, the difference between the current tool length and the programmed tool length is used to adjust the vertical axis of the machine when it is running a program. In this way, the final accuracy depends on your ability to measure accurately and your ability to transfer that data to the proper field in the tool table.

While this is an improvement over the purely mechanical efforts, it does require knowledge, judgement and skill. Again, we need to find a way around the requirement for these things.

The answer is automatic tool measurement. This system uses a measurement button located off the rear of the table. The new tool is moved over the button and then lowered until it contacts the button. The new length is then determined by the position of the Z axis and this new value is input into the tool table. This entire process, positioning, measuring and entering the data is totally automatic. Again, these systems are commercially available and being shipped today.

We have now touched on the various requirements for near zero setup. We have looked at fixture design and changing fixtures. We have discussed fixture verification, tooling selection, measurement and management.

Now, we are going to turn our attention to some of the actual machining and operating requirements of furniture fabrication. The first general requirement is that all processes needed to build a piece of furniture be performed within the cell. This is not an absolute necessity, but, the more it is followed, the more competitive the process becomes.

Certain processes, leg carving for example, are better performed on a specialized multi-spindle machine rather than directly in the cell. In these instances, the leg carvings need to be processed independently and then the carved part added to the material kit before the kit is moved to the fabrication cell. If too much material is handled in this manner, however, most of the cost advantages of the fabrication cell will be lost.

The CNC router is the major piece of equipment within the cell and thus it will perform that vast majority of the work. However, it is not necessarily going to perform everything that is done in the cell. In determining how a process is to be performed, simple common sense should prevail.

For example, it would be much more practical to perform edge banding by using a small separate edge bander next to the machine than to try and incorporate edge banding on the router itself. From a technical standpoint, I have seen edge banding performed on CNC machines, even on curved surfaces. From a practical standpoint, however, it might make more sense to have the cell operator hand feed a simple edge bander while the CNC machine is cutting other parts.

Each individual case will vary and it will be necessary to judge and decide which operations should be performed on the CNC machine and which should be performed on other machines in the cell. One of the most important factors in making this decision is whether or not the peripheral machines need to be set up for different parts. Any machines that require special setup between parts should normally not be considered for secondary operations.

At the same time, you do not want a cycle where the CNC machine is performing all the work and the cell operator has nothing to do except watch the machine. The ideal situation is where the CNC machine is busy all the time and the cell operator is also performing useful work through most of the cycle.

Therefore we want to find tasks for the cell operator that use machines that do not require setup for different parts and we want to find enough of these tasks so that the operator is kept reasonably busy. At the same time, we do not want the machine waiting for the cell operator to complete his or her tasks because the amount of work required is just too much for the time available.

Even simple tasks, like drilling a hole, which the CNC machine is quite capable of performing might be better done off line if, for example, a separate tool might be required. It might take more time to stop, change tools, drill one hole and then change back to another tool than it would take to simply drill the hole off line using a locating fixture. This might also be true if the part needs to be relocated to drill a single hole.

At the same time, we must consider the fact that a hole drilled by the machine will, most likely, be more accurately located than a hole drilled off line. If the accuracy of placement of the hole is important to the alignment or assembly, it might make more sense to use the CNC machine. These decisions must be made on a case by case basis. What makes sense in one instance might be totally wrong in another.

Another change from traditional manufacturing on a CNC router is that in furniture fabrication, we may need to reorient a part several times to completely machine it. The most common way to machine a part on a CNC router is to locate it and then perform all operations in one setup. If horizontal machining is required, a horizontally oriented head is used. If a part is to be sawed, a saw head in the proper orientation is used or, perhaps, a saw head that can be oriented by the program.

The main problem with this approach is that the type of parts that the machine can process is limited by the mechanical head configuration of the machine. For furniture fabrication, a wide variety of different parts must be machined. To accomplish this, a flexible head configuration is required and then the parts may need to be oriented to allow the existing head to perform the necessary operations.

A good example of this is the vertical side table. This is a table mounted at a ninety-degree angle to the main horizontal machine table. Normally it extends from one edge of the table downward toward the floor. Its primary use is to mount a panel so that its edge is pointed straight upward. In this way, the standard automatic tool change spindle can be used to perform special edge work such as dovetailing.

Normally, this type of work would be performed by positioning the part horizontally on some type of fixture flat on the tabletop. The edge is then machined using a special horizontal head. The problem with this approach is that I am not aware of a horizontal head that allows for an automatic tool changer. Thus, unless you are willing to restrict the head to one tool, you will require a manual tool change between parts. You will also restrict the edge work to only one tool per head per cycle since tool changing is not an option.

By using the standard tool-change vertical head, a variety of different work can be performed on the edge of a panel and you no longer are restricted to one tool. The machine is simpler, lower cost and the flexibility is much greater. The only requirement is that the parts must be oriented differently.

This same logic applies to machining different surfaces of a part. In most cases it will be easier to rotate and remount the part than to try and develop a series of special heads to machine the part in a single orientation.

I have been surprised at how much resistance there is to simply rotating or reorienting the part during the cycle. I have seen companies spend tens of thousands of extra dollars to configure a machine so that the part would not need to be reoriented. Perhaps this makes sense if you are running thousands of parts at a time. When you are running only one or two pieces at a time in furniture fabrication, it is extremely practical to reorient the piece, possibly several times to allow the machine to attack the piece in the simplest possible orientation.

The most common process you will encounter in furniture fabrication is routing. When you mention CNC routers, this is obviously what people think of. Routing is, however an extremely flexible process.

Tool bit technology has been advancing rapidly. This is adding to the capability as well as the flexibility available from the routing process. Special tools are now available for everything from high speed machining of plywood and MDF to hardwood tools that minimize tear out and produce smooth finished edges. This advancing technology will continue into the future, further increasing capability.

The key to the routing process is the ability to use the proper tool for the proper job. This means that a selection of tools and a fast tool change system are a necessity. It is also necessary that the machine be able to store and automatically retrieve all the tools that are required for all parts. We have already talked about bulk tool changers and tool management.

Although I have described Thermwood's approach to this requirement, there may be other valid methods of handling the tooling requirement. I understand that other companies also offer bulk tool storage and automatic tool change capability and these may very well meet the requirements. Thermwood has filed for patent protection on the concept of an at-the-head tool changer interacting with a bulk tool changer so this particular approach may not be available from multiple vendors. It is likely, however, that there are other approaches that will satisfy this need.

As we look at other wood machining processes, you will find that many of those will actually be variations of the routing process. As we examine each of these processes, we will focus on the result of the process and then determine how to achieve that same result using a CNC router. The process itself, mortise and tenon for example, may actually be accomplished today using different tools and techniques. In furniture fabrication we will not necessarily try and use exactly the same tools and techniques but instead, we will try and achieve the same final result using the machine and tools available.

Shaping is very similar to routing, at least the final result is quite similar. Both processes machine a contour or shape to the edge of a part or panel. Routers use router bits with an integral center shaft and tend to operate at relatively high speeds. Shapers generally use a shaper head, which has a hole through the center. This head mounts to the drive shaft of the shaper motor. Some shaper heads have the shaped knives permanently attached to the head while others have replaceable knives. Shapers generally rotate at a slower speed than routers, are larger in diameter and are generally used for heavier cross sections than a router.

There are really two approaches to shaping on a CNC router. The first is to mount a shaper head on the machine. There are both pluses and minuses to this simple approach. As a general rule of thumb, a shaper head will result in a smoother profile than a router bit, simply because the diameter of the shaper tends to be much larger than the diameter of the router bit. Normal tooling marks, the marks caused by the individual flutes or knives, tend to be less noticeable with the larger diameter shaper head. At the same time, you must realize that the edge will need to be sanded before finishing whether you are shaping or routing. In general, it will require essentially the same sanding effort in either case.

The real advantage of the shaper is that it can generally cut a larger profile than a router. It can also normally remove more material in a single pass than a router.

A router, however, is a second approach to generating a shaped edge. The router will not be able to easily reproduce all shapes that a shaper can cut. There is normally a limit to the diameter router bit that can be run in a particular spindle. If the depth of the shape is greater than the maximum router bit diameter, it may be either difficult or impossible to substitute a router for a shaper.

In many other circumstances, however, it is possible to machine an edge, normally associated with a shaper, by using one or more router bits. Sometimes, two or more router bits are required with each machining a portion of the final shape. This does require additional time but offers some advantages.

First, it is possible to use both right hand and left hand rotating router bits by simply changing tools and reversing the direction of rotation of the router spindle. When machining some materials, certain areas may require right hand rotation and others may require left hand rotation to avoid tearing out the material. To accommodate this requirement using a shaper will generally require two shaper heads, one with right hand rotation and one with left hand rotation.

Also, router tooling can be changed automatically quite easily. Shaper tooling, at least today, cannot be automatically changed quite as easily. Although this may change in the future, today, shaper heads will need to be changed by hand. If the number of pieces that require shaping is small, it may take longer to change shaper tools than to simply machine the part in two or more passes using router tooling which does not require manual changing.

Shaper heads are readily available on CNC routers. The decision as to whether to add the shaper head or to use the router head to achieve the required shapes is based on all the above factors. In some instances it will make more sense to use separate shaper heads and in others it might make sense to use the router head.

A third alternative is to use both. If all your shapes use a relatively common base section with variations occurring in a detail area, it might make sense to use a common shaper to cut the base profile for all shaped parts and then use different shaped router bits to achieve the individual designs. In this way, you can realize the major benefits of both systems without the need to change shaper heads between parts.

Most of what we said about shaping also goes for molding. Molder knives and shaper knives tend to be somewhat similar. The final result of molding is essentially shaping a long straight part. In molding, a straight piece of material is fed through the machine, which puts a shape on one, or more, faces of the piece.

When molding with a CNC router, the piece is does not feed through the machine. Instead, the piece is rigidly mounted and the shaper or router head passes across the piece putting the necessary shape on the face of the part.

If the piece requires more than one face to be molded, it is generally necessary to mold one face and then rotate the part, either within the current fixture or to another fixture, so that another face can be machined. Granted, this is slower than simply feeding the piece through a molder. If you consider the time required to mount the proper knives and set up the molder, the CNC router may very well be faster overall, especially if the number of pieces being cut is small.

If only a few molded pieces are required, there is another way to cut a molding that does not even require a special router bit or knife. This technique uses a ball nosed router bit and cuts the molding like a long straight carving. The tool moves back and forth indexing a small distance each pass until it cuts the entire shape. This doesn't take nearly as long as you might think and is quite practical for larger profiles.

The photo to the right is a part of a Bombay base for a clock. It is essentially a very wide molding that was machined using this technique. This technique allowed the machining of this piece without the need  for special molding knives and without the need for a large and expensive molding machine. The volume requirement for this part was quite low so the extra time needed to make the piece was a small price to pay for the substantial tooling and machine savings.

Boring or drilling holes is another common process. Although the practice of simply adding one or more drill heads is the most common way to bore, it is not the only choice.

If the product requires extensive boring, adding a multi spindle boring head might actually be a reasonable choice. If you have a series of holes located on 32mm centers, it might make sense to add a multi-spindle boring head and drill several holes at the same time. This seems to make a lot of sense but many times it is not the most efficient way to line bore.

The factor that determines how holes are to be bored is the variety of sizes that may be needed. If a single diameter hole is required on all furniture made, then this straightforward approach is probably the most efficient. If, however, different sized holes are required for different pieces, or even on the same piece, then a different approach is required.

When tooling a machine for boring, the primary goal is to provide for boring every hole that will ever be needed without the need to change drill bits. You should not need to change drill bits within a part and you should not be required to change drill bits when changing to a new part.

This is an extremely important consideration. It may look almost trivial to simply change one or two drill bits between parts and, in fact, it is. The real problem is not the simple task of changing bits, it is that the entire changeover process must be modified in order to change a single tool. Once a procedure is in place to control manual tool changes, our near zero changeover advantage is lost.

Until now we have been describing a system where the machine automatically selects tools, measures the tools and verifies the fixture. The operator has not needed any knowledge of tooling or configuration in order to change from building one piece to another.

Once the operator is asked to change a bit, a whole new level of knowledge, skill and discipline is required. You need to know which bit to change, which diameter goes into which spindle. A system is needed to transmit this information. You need to know how to measure and verify bit diameter. You need to make sure the length is correct. You need to know what correct length is.

The worst thing is that now, human judgement has been added to the system so human error is possible. To avoid human error, checks must be added to the procedure. As you can see, an entire level of complexity is being added just so we can accommodate bit changes.

In some circumstances this may be unavoidable, however, if the choice is to bore holes one at a time and not require bit changes or bore holes in groups and change bits, the one-at-a-time approach is the clear winner. It may take slightly longer to bore holes one at a time, however, after your system evolves with all the quality checks and balances needed to accommodate manual tool changes, it will likely take less time to drill holes one at a time than to accomplish and check the bit change.

This is a very important concept. Once you begin adding layers of judgement and control to the process, the whole thing will degrade and deteriorate until it is no better off than today's operations. The key to real profits is to keep things simple. Sometimes, keeping things simple may require operations that appear less efficient. They are really not less efficient when you consider the enormous cost of allowing additional complexity to invade your operation.

I have suggested to many companies that they equip their nine spindle drill bank with every diameter drill bit from 1/16 inch to 7/16 inch, plus a countersink and a counterbore. In this way, one drill bank can drill every hole size required without the need for tool changes. The ½ inch hole can be cut using a ½ inch router bit. Holes larger than ½ inch can be cut using the same router bit by simply defining very small circles.

This arrangement can bore virtually every size hole ever required without the need to ever change bits between parts. When dull bits need to be changed, it is simply necessary to change each bit with the exact same diameter bit, a relatively easy task that requires no real detailed information about which bit goes in which spindle.

There are a couple of considerations about using a router bit to bore holes. First, if you plan to bore holes by plunging the router bit into the material you will require a plunge tip bit. All router bits are not made with cutting edges that extend across the entire bottom of the tool. If you plan to bore, you will need router bits designed to cut with the bottom as well as the side.

If you try and bore with a non-plunge tip router bit, you will likely succeed, but at a price. The CNC router will normally exert enough force that some non-plunge tip bits can actually create holes. The problem is that it will require a substantial axial load to push the tool through the material. This will quickly destroy your spindle since most spindles are not designed for heavy axial loads. Even spindles such as Thermwood's Extended Duty Router, which are designed specifically to handle excess axial loads will eventually fail prematurely if subjected to constant excessive axial loads caused by plunging with a non-plunge tip bit.

Plunging with a non-plunge tip bit will also develop excessive heat. This heat will also shorten spindle life and may also reduce tool bit life.

The second consideration when making holes with a router bit concerns those instances where we are trying to create slightly larger holes by machining very small diameter circles. While this should work very well in theory, in practice, some well known CNC controls break down when asked to create a very small diameter circle. The actual circle created in these instances can be quite crude. I have seen these types of small circles look more like triangles or squares than circles.

I am mentioning this because this problem, which was common with early CNC controls, still exists. Most, but not all, current CNC controls calculate circles with high enough precision that they are round at any radius. If you plan to use this technique for developing holes, you need to make certain that the control you plan to run is capable of producing acceptable small diameter circles.

Now that we have discussed drilling holes on the CNC router, I will add another idea to further complicate the discussion. In furniture fabrication, it may make more sense to drill at least some of the holes off-line than to drill them as part of the machine cycle.

This may sound like heresy to some who want technology to solve all their problems, automatically. In fact, many times this can be the most efficient way to perform the operation, especially if there is some special aspect to the holes.

An example of this was seen on the furniture fabrication cell we developed to produce a carved, solid wood wall table. We used screws to attach the tabletop to the frame and legs. To do this we used counterbored pilot holes that were drilled at an angle from the inside of the table frame into the tabletop. This operation had several problems.

First, the holes were drilled at an angle so a simple vertical drill head could not be used. Their location was not critical except that we needed a certain number to hold the top on properly.

In order to perform this operation on the machine we would have needed special lift fixtures to orient the tabletop so that the holes could be drilled at the proper angle. Instead, we used a simple, commercially available drill fixture and hand drilled the holes during the assembly process. The operator had plenty of time to do this and the machine cycle was both simpler and faster.

Boring is one of those tasks that, with the proper fixtures, can be performed off the machine. The guiding principal here is to determine what is the most practical simplest way to perform the job. If hole location is critical, it is probably better to drill the hole on the machine. If, on the other hand, hole location is not critical or other factors are present, such as drilling at an odd angle, manual drilling might make sense.

This same principal applies to all the operations. There is no reason not to consider performing an operation using a simple manual machine if it simplifies the machine cycle and can be performed easily and reliably.

Mortise and tenon construction has been popular with furniture builders almost from the beginning of time. It offers strong reliable joints that can be machined or cut into the actual members themselves.

Normally, the mortise is cut using a mortise machine with a chisel mortise. The chisel mortise consists of a hollow square chisel with a large rotating bit running in the center of the chisel. As the chisel mortise moves downward through the material, the rotating bit removes the vast majority of material from the center. The square chisel cuts the edges and corners, pushing material into the bit where it is removed.

This approach requires considerable force to operate and it may be necessary to back up the face of the part to keep the impression of the mortise from telegraphing through to the outer surface.

Many years ago, we were told that the industry wanted this type of mortise put on a CNC router. We designed and built a system that used a chisel mortise on our machines, and we offered these to the market. We only sold one or two of them, because the market decided that they could just machine the mortise hole using a small router bit and an "H" pattern. The resulting hole looked like this:

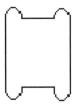

You will notice that the hole isn't exactly square, however, by overshooting at the corners, the round inside corners do not interfere with the square tenon.

For this type of traditional mortise and tenon, the tenon is cut on the edge of the mating part using a tenon machine. A wide saw blade or other type of cutter is run over all four sides creating a square tenon that mates with the mortise.

In order to accommodate this square shape when cutting the mortise with a router bit, the "H" shape is required.

This approach has the obvious advantage that a more-or-less square hole can be machined using a standard router bit. This eliminates the need for a special square hole mortise head.

The disadvantage of this approach, however, is that the mortise and tenon do not touch at all points. The four areas where the relief was machined do not contact. This means that, at least in theory, the strength of the joint is not as good as a standard square hole mortise.

For furniture fabrication purposes, mortise and tenon construction is quite important. The major constraint for traditional mortise and tenon construction is that the tenon is square because of the

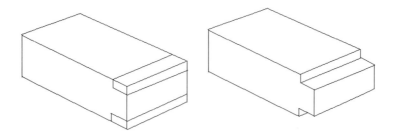

way it is cut. The tenon is cut by removing material from two opposing sides, or from all four sides of a part. This is generally done on a tenoning machine where the part is moved past cutting heads that remove the material.

As you can see by the above sketch, the resulting tenon has square edges that require a square mortise for a solid fit.

One real advantage of cutting a tenon using a router is that the tenon shape no longer needs to be square. Using a router bit to cut the tenon allows you to cut a tenon that has a round edge that can exactly match the hole cut by a router bit.

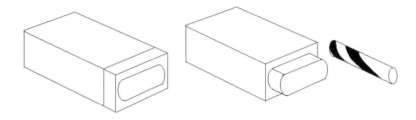

There are two ways to cut this tenon on a CNC router. The first, and most obvious is to use a horizontal head and orient the part horizontally as shown above. The second method is to orient the part vertically on a vertical machine table and then cut the tenon using the main router head. This second method has some advantages but also has some limitations.

It has the advantage of not requiring a separate horizontal head. Horizontal heads generally rotate slower than standard router spindles, so cutting is somewhat slower. Also, horizontal heads do not generally have the ability to automatically change tools so you are stuck with a single tool for this application, although normally this is not a problem.

The real disadvantage of orienting the part vertically is that the length of the part is limited. If the part gets too long, it will hit the floor. For parts oriented horizontally, there is no real limit to their length. Parts considerably longer than the machine table can be cut provided the portion that extends beyond the table is supported by a simple roller conveyor.

One other aspect of cutting a mortise and tenon using a CNC router must be understood. There is a tendency to simply assume that you will cut the mortise by plunging the router bit and cutting a slot in a single pass using the diameter of the router bit to define the width of the slot. You will then create a path to cut the tenon to match the diameter of the router bit. Therein lies the problem.

You don't know what the diameter of the router bit really is. Normal commercial router bits can vary several thousandths in diameter. Although this doesn't sound like much, variances can cause serious assembly problems. If the mortise tool were three thousandths small it would cut the mortise three thousandths undersized. If the tool cutting the tenon were also three thousandths small it would cut the tenon three thousandths oversize. You now have a six-thousandths error.

If the planned clearance were less than six thousandths the parts are not going to fit together without a lot of encouragement.

The obvious solution is to make the fit greater than the maximum variation you expect to encounter so that regardless of the tool variations the parts will always fit together. The downside of this approach is that when the tools are oversized, the parts are six thousandths undersized. Add this to the six or eight thousandths planned clearance and you have twelve to fourteen thousands slop. This is a loose, relatively poor joint.

The proper approach is to use the machine's tool radius compensation. CNC routers have the ability to adjust the program path to allow for variations in the actual tool diameter versus the programmed diameter. To use this feature, however, proper commands need to be added to the program. If the tool is two thousandths undersized, the control will move it two thousandths closer to the part giving an accurate cut even though the tool is the wrong size.

You can see how this would work with the tenon, but we will need to modify the program for the mortise. Because the diameter of the tool will vary, we will not be able to simply cut a single slot with the tool. Instead, we will need to cut one side of the slot using one edge of the tool and then cut the opposite side of the slot using the other edge of the tool. Then as the tool diameter varies, the control can shift the program toward or away from the edges of the slot assuring that the width of the slot is always accurate.

This is a simple but important concept. To make furniture fabrication work, you must recognize that many things will vary from tooling to stock thickness. Each of these possible variations must be dealt with in the way the cell is programmed. There is a natural tendency to solve variation problems by simply tightening up tolerances. If stock varies too much for proper assembly, accept less variation from the rough mill or your supplier.

This is almost always the wrong approach. It adds cost, since we now need tighter tolerances. It adds QC inspections, additional rejects, more paperwork, and a less reliable source of material.

It is much better to use the technology of the machine to handle variations. If the tool varies, compensate for the variation. If the material varies, either measure and compensate for the variation or develop assembly methods that do not rely on raw material dimensions. We will cover part measurement a little later in this chapter.

The next process we will cover is sawing. Almost every CNC router manufacturer offers some type of saw option. In traditional furniture manufacturing, sawing parts is a fairly common process. Sawing in furniture fabrication is somewhat less common.

Much of furniture fabrication is nested base. This means that parts are nested together and cut from a large sheet of material. The common method of separating a sheet of material into individual panels is with a panel saw. Stacks of material can be cut up into various sized panels rather quickly.

Since furniture fabrication is not running with a traditional batch, only a single sheet of material will generally be cut up at a time. Also, the sheet will need to be cut up while lying flat on the tabletop. Normally this will be done using a router bit rather than a saw. The saw blade has the advantage that the saw kerf is less than the kerf left by a router bit. Theoretically the yield might be slightly better.

In practice, the slightly larger kerf left by the router bit will seldom decrease yield and, parts can be nested more efficiently using a router bit. To use a saw blade on a fixed panel, the saw must move from one edge of the sheet all the way through to the other edge of the sheet. It is not practical to stop the blade in the center of the panel because the top edge of the blade has cut farther than the bottom edge.

This means that the parts must be oriented so that all the edges line up with each other so that they can be cut with a saw. At best, this will reduce yield and in many instances it is simply not possible to break the panel apart without removing and replacing panels during the process.

For these reasons, use of a saw in panel processing is restricted to other applications. There are times when a thin groove or slot is required and a saw blade is the best alternative.

A saw blade with a horizontal router bit in the center is an ideal tool for frame or five piece door building.

In this application, the saw blade is stopped and positioned as a fixed stop to locate and clamp the material. Although we are showing the blade itself being used as a locator, a guard in front of the blade can also be used as the part locator stop. This guard will generally flex less and provide a more accur5ate positioning than using the saw blade itself.

Once the stock has been inserted to the proper depth, the saw then cuts off the piece to the proper length. The center router bit can then be used to machine tenons or other edge treatments.

Solid wood carvings tend to separate fairly high end furniture from lower cost, simpler products. Carving can actually be done in a furniture fabrication cell, but there are several important considerations. First, however, let us examine how carving is completed on a CNC router.

Carving is the process that separates the truly capable machines from the rest. There are some key requirements for a CNC router to be able to carve and all but a few of the top end machines don't have these capabilities.

Carving with a CNC router borrows many techniques from carving with a hand operated multi-spindle carver. It is a multi-step process. The first step is roughing where a larger diameter tool is moved over the raw blank to develop the basic shape and structure of the carved part.

After the roughing pass, a smaller diameter tool, generally with a flat bottom, is used to develop the square bottom corners of the carving. This is commonly called the squaring tool. Then a fine pointed tool is used to create the detail lines in the carving. This tool is generally referred to as the liner tool.

Some carving may require additional tools to achieve the desired final result, but, most carvings can be completed with three to four different tools.

There are essentially two different types of carvings. Flat parts include door and drawer fronts and similar pieces. Three dimensional carvings include chair legs, table legs, bed posts and the like.

These two different types of carvings are generally done on two different types of machines. Flat work carvings are commonly done on standard routers with one or two heads while three dimensional carvings are generally done on a carving router. If the flat work carving is less than about 10 inches in one dimension, it can be done, six at a time, on a carving router fitted with flat worktables.

When carvings are added to a product a decision must be made as to how and where that carving function is to be done. Carvings significantly increase the time required to complete a part. Simple, limited area carvings can generally be accomplished with little increase in cycle time. Extensive carvings, however, can quickly become the dominant factor in production rates. The decision as to how and where to perform carvings must be made on a product by product basis.

As an example, the baroque grandfather clock we made for a trade show consisted of a large, and elaborate, carved front door. In addition, the Bombay style base was cut using carving techniques. In this particular example, the overall production cycle was over eight and a half hours. Of this, all but about twenty minutes was carving.

In this case, the sanding and finish effort required virtually the entire period so the operator was kept busy doing useful work. The final product was quite expensive, so it made sense to tie up the cell for almost nine hours producing one item. At the same time, you can see that high volume production involving extensive carving will require a large number of cells.

If carved legs are required, it may make more sense to carve the legs, six at a time on a separate carving router and then add the carved legs to the material kits before the fabrication cell begins working on the product. Either the material kits are routed through the carving shop before they are placed in raw material storage or the carving can be performed at the rough mill where the material kits are first assembled.

The advantage of using the carving router is that six parts are carved at the same time, versus carving one part at a time in the fabrication cell. The disadvantage is that it adds an additional step to the production process with all the associated problems and inefficiencies.

If carving is to be part of the final product, the decision as to where and how to do the carving must be approached and addressed carefully. It may even be necessary to perform some of the carving in a separate carving shop and some of it at the cell itself.

If a substantial amount of carving is to be part of the product line, an off-line carving capability will certainly be necessary for at least part of the requirements. Once this capability is in place, the selection of where to perform the production carving will need to be made based on actual experience. In making the selection, however, be certain to try and consider the disruptions caused by the necessity of coordinating a separate carving effort with the operation of the fabrication cell.

A final comment on carving is a caution. As this book is being written, all CNC routers are not capable of carving. In fact, only three systems I am aware of have actually performed carving on a production basis. To perform carving requires a fairly high performance CNC control and a servo system with little or no lead/lag error. The majority of CNC routers today do not have this combination of capabilities. If you will require carving, make certain that you base your fabrication cell on a machine that is actually capable of carving.

The next process we will cover is dovetailing. Dovetail construction is a common process in higher quality furniture. It is commonly used for drawer construction. Dovetails can be machined on a CNC router, both the end dovetails such as those used for drawer construction as well as the long French dovetails used to join two panels at right angles to one another.

Dovetails are not a particularly easy process for most factories today. The reason for this is that size is very important and the accuracy required to make dovetails fit properly is quite high. This is an area where CNC router technology can take a process that is normally troublesome and make it relatively easy to perform.

The reason that dovetails can be cut on CNC routers easily is the variables, which cause problems, can be identified and handled by the technology of the system.

Before we discuss the methods used to machine dovetails, let us examine some of the variables that can cause problems.

A typical method of cutting dovetails is to use a dovetail guide and a dovetail cutter bit. This guide defines the path that the dovetail cutter will take in cutting the dovetails. The result is exactly the same as if the path were defined by a CNC router rather than a physical guide.

The variable that can cause problems in this application is the diameter of the dovetail cutter. Router bits are not perfect and this includes dovetail cutters. They are generally manufactured to relatively tight tolerances, a few thousandths of an inch for example. The problem lies in that any variation in diameter is doubled in this application. For example, if the cutter were three thousandths undersized, it would cut the male portion of the dovetail three thousandths over sized. It would also cut the female portion of the dovetail three thousandths undersized.

When you try and assemble this dovetail joint, you are trying to fit a part that is too big into a hole that is too small. The difference is six thousandths, which is quite a bit. A large hammer and some serious effort and you might be able to get the parts together but it is less than ideal.

If the cutter were oversized rather than undersized, the problem would be a loose fit and a poor quality joint. To make dovetails properly, they must be more accurate than the tool itself.

Fortunately, this is relatively easy for a CNC router. We begin by developing a program that will result in a perfect fit if the tool were exactly the correct size. We then measure the real diameter of the tool being used and supply this information to a tool radius compensation system within the control. The control then shifts the program to allow for the difference in the tool diameter. The result is better quality dovetails than are possible with mechanical guides.

There are some logistic concerns in cutting these types of dovetails that we should cover. The female portion of the dovetail can be easily cut by laying the part flat on the tabletop. The male portion, however, requires that the dovetail be cut on the edge of the part. If the part is also laid flat, this will require a horizontal spindle. It will also require that the part be raised far enough above the table to provide clearance for the horizontal spindle assembly. This somewhat complicates the situation.

An easier solution is to equip the machine table with a small, second table that is vertical rather than horizontal. We normally place these along, and at ninety degrees to the edge of the main machine table.

The part to be machined can now be mounted so that the edge to be machined is pointed straight up. This allows the main head to perform the dovetail machining. This main head is also equipped with an automatic tool changer so this arrangement offers substantial flexibility in performing work on the edge of a part.

If the machine does not have a permanent vertical table, a removable table can be fabricated. This table is normally built in an "L" shape. The top of the "L" is secured to the standard table top using screws, clamps or vacuum. The side of "L" then protrudes vertically toward the floor providing a simple vertical table for holding parts.

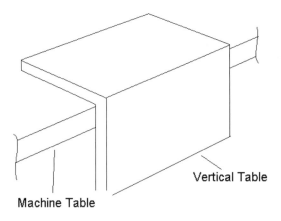

Vertical Table

Machine Table

Removable Vertical Table

The only real disadvantage to vertical tables is that the overall length of the part being machined is limited to the distance from the cutting head to the floor since the part is oriented vertically. If longer parts need edge machining, it may be necessary to use a horizontal router, however, you will give up the flexibility of an automatic tool changer. You may also need to change tools manually when you change from one part to another. If at all possible, you should try to avoid this requirement.

A second type of dovetail is the long, sliding joint, sometimes referred as a French dovetail. This assembly method is seldom used today because it is quite difficult to achieve on a production basis. It was used in the past when each joint was cut and fitted manually.

Again, this type of joint can be reliably machined on a CNC router, but there are some additional considerations.

The concerns about cutter diameter apply to this joint just as with the other type of dovetail, and the problem is solved in the same manner. The depth of the dovetail is a second concern that must also be addressed. To provide for a tight, strong joint that does not bind during assembly, the depth of the dovetail slot must be maintained very accurately. The important depth is the distance from the face of the panel to the bottom of the dovetail.

Problems occur because the machine cuts a precise distance from the tabletop, which is also the back of the panel being cut, not the front. If the thickness of the panel varies, this variation shows up as a variation in the depth of the dovetail.

In normal operation, panel thickness is not maintained accurately enough to cut acceptable dovetails in the front face. Some method must be used to allow for variation in panel thickness.

There are two methods by which this can be done. First, a router with a floating head can be used to cut the dovetail. This is a router that is free to move up and down a small distance. It has a slide plate at the bottom that rides on the panel being machined. The cutter protrudes a set distance through the slide plate and this sets the depth of the cut. While this system can work, it presents several problems.

First, it requires a special floating head, which will not normally be equipped with an automatic tool changer. It also requires that the tool depth be very accurately adjusted mechanically. Anytime an analog mechanical adjustment is required, the opportunity for error exists and people with special skills are required. Also, certain materials can be scratched by the slide plate and sawdust from other operations can get under the slide plate and cause depth errors.

Another method for adjusting for part thickness variations is to measure each part using a sensor attached to the machine head. This sensor tells the control the exact thickness of the part. This actual thickness can be compared to the programmed thickness and the program can be adjusted automatically to compensate for the variation.

If the part thickness varies but the overall thickness is consistent, a single measurement may be sufficient. If the part might be slightly wedge shaped, it may require a separate measurement at each end of the cut. It is even possible to take several measurements along the cut and create a path that exactly compensates for thickness variations, however, this may add some additional problems.

In this case, the path would not be a straight line but would be curved to match the curved upper surface of the part. It may be difficult to impossible to assemble a straight dovetail from one part to the curved dovetail on the other. This same effect would occur if a floating head is used to cut a dovetail into a panel whose top surface was wavy.

One advantage of making just two measurements at each end of the slot and then cutting a straight dovetail from one to the other is that, even with a wavy part, you machine a straight dovetail that will be easy to assemble. In this case, both ends will be true and tight but variations and problems may occur in the center of the cut.

I believe that a sensor is a fundamental requirement of a furniture fabrication cell. This is just one example of how this type of sensor can be used.

A key concept for furniture fabrication is to expect incoming variation and to design the cell and programming to handle any possible variation in the normal course of operation. The two most common ways of handling this variation is to either make all critical cuts on the CNC router or measure the exact dimension and adjust the program for the true size.

Another key component that is necessary to make all this work is the Advanced Function Language. Normal CNC code is not able to handle measurements and is not able to automatically adjust for variations. To accomplish these things requires additional program commands and capabilities. These additional commands and capabilities are available in an expanded instruction set that Thermwood calls the Advanced Function Language.

We will discuss this capability further later in this book.

The final process we will cover is sanding. As a general rule, you will not be able to route or shape wood components smoothly enough that they do not require sanding. The surface left by a cutting process, such as routing, is different than the surface that results from sanding. Even if the surface quality from the routing or shaping process was smooth enough, it will take the finish differently than the sanded parts of the component unless it is also sanded.

Sanding is another process where you will need to decide whether to sand using the machine or to sand as a separate operation off the machine. I will start by describing the current state of machine sanding technology and then I will address the question of where to sand.

When we talk about sanding on a CNC router, we are generally talking about sanding a routed or shaped edge profile. The CNC router has the advantage that it can sand edges that are not straight such as a curved profile edge.

I am aware of three different systems that have successfully sanded profile edges on a CNC router. Each relies to some extent on the ability of the machine to cut the edge and then very accurately sand the edge.

The first system uses a plastic sanding disk that is formed to the exact contour of the edge. The system consists of both the shaper and the sanding head since the match between the two must be very accurate.

The shaper knives used in this process must be very accurate. In fact, the required accuracy is beyond that normally required and therefore few knife suppliers can fabricate the required shape. To operate properly and achieve acceptable sanding media life, a match within a few thousandths of an inch across the entire shape is required. Achieving this accuracy is not simple.

Many things that are taken for granted in woodworking must be handled with precision. Even something as simple as mounting the shaper blades requires a special ground fixture to assure that the blades are perfectly square and accurate. The sanding media holder is machined to within less than a thousandth of an inch and special precision collapsing mandrels are needed to assure that the sanding media rotates perfectly.

The goal in all this is to remove between three and five thousandths on an inch of material each pass. This provides the best balance between material removal and media life. If you draw a line across the profile with a lead pencil, one sanding pass will remove most of the line but you will still see a trace of the line. The remaining trace should be completely even in density if the system is working properly.

Obviously, for this system to work properly the CNC router must repeat very accurately. Repeating dynamically within this tolerance range is not a trivial feat. The technical hurdles required to accomplish this are substantial and I would venture that few commercial CNC routers would qualify. At the time this is being written we have been able to achieve acceptable results in demonstrations and shows but have only sold a few of these systems and we are not certain that they are being used on a production basis.

A second system that we have not had as much experience with ( but understand is being used in production on other machines) uses a special metal head that has been machined to the appropriate shape. To this is attached sanding pads that perform the actual sanding operation. We have been told that this system does not require quite the high level of accuracy and can remove substantially more material per pass. We do not know how easily the media loads up nor what can be expected in media life.

A third system uses a special solid precision sanding tool that fits into the router spindle. This tool is solid steel, machined to exactly match the profile of the router bit that cuts the edge profile. This solid tool is then coated with a diamond abrasive.

This system works very similar to the first system described, removing three to five thousandths per pass. It requires the same precision, but this level of precision is somewhat easier to achieve since we are using a solid, one-piece router bit and a solid sanding tool. If the two tools are machined accurately, the match up is much easier to achieve. Obviously with the diamond abrasive, tool life should be very long. The other advantage is that it does not require a special sanding spindle. A single router spindle with an automatic tool changer can be used to both route and sand although the speed must be reduced for sanding.

We have demonstrated this sanding head at trade shows and it does work. We have even reversed the spindle and sanded in one direction and then the other providing quite a nice edge. Unfortunately few people noticed what we were doing and we have seen little interest in this process. At this point, the only tools of this type that I am aware of are two experimental systems we have used here at Thermwood.

This brings us back to the fundamental question as to whether sanding on the machine makes sense. For the systems described here, it will generally take two passes to obtain an acceptable edge finish. Each of these passes will be slower than the cutting pass so sanding will require a reasonable amount of machine time.

Although we have done some machine sanding for our demonstration cells, currently we would opt to sand off-line by hand. Although this may take even more time than machine sanding, the operator will generally have more than enough time perform this operation during assembly. Generally the machine cycle will become the factor that limits production. This is one area where we can reduce that machine time and easily perform the task by hand.

Although this is my current recommendation, there may be times where automatic edge profile sanding makes sense. Should you decide to go this way, realize that this technology is somewhat new and some experimentation and development may be needed.

These are the basic processes that are performed on a CNC router. There are several additional processes that may be needed, however, normally these are better performed within the cell but off the machine.

I have seen edge banding demonstrated on a CNC router but the system looks both complex and slow. The process I witnessed attached two layers of relatively thick edge banding to a curved part and then cut a mild shape into the edge. The result was quite nice but did require a fairly long cycle.

For normal edge banding applications I still believe that performing these off-line will be more efficient. Like any guide, however, this is not always the case so you must examine your application very carefully to determine the best way to perform this function.

Another area where I have strong personal feelings has to do with adhesives. I favor the expensive hot applied urethane systems. These offer extremely strong joints, can be formulated to provide the necessary working time and, are fast. This last feature, fast, is the key.

These adhesives can set up in as little as thirty seconds to a minute. In most applications, special clamping or holding fixtures are not needed. The parts are simply aligned, held in place until the adhesive starts to set and the job is done.

These adhesives are more expensive than other alternatives. This cost must be balanced against the cost of clamping fixtures, additional assembly time and the clutter of assembled parts sitting around drying. To make a fabrication cell work at all, glue set-up time must be less than the overall production cycle time, sometimes much less. If the production cycle is short, a half hour or so, you may be limited in the adhesives that will work anyway.

In some cases it may be possible to screw or pin nail the piece together to hold it in place until the adhesive sets. The only potential problem with this approach is that the assembled components will be further assembled into the finished piece and then the finished piece moved to finishing before the adhesive is fully cured. This opens up a lot of possibility for breaking or weakening the glue joint. This means that for a few cents in adhesive cost you could end up with a poor quality end product.

Considering the overall savings available from this process, a little additional cost to use a faster better adhesive is well worth the investment.

There are some other associated technologies that should be mentioned. We have referred to part measurement several times already. Exactly what is part measurement and how does it work?

Part measurement is a combination of hardware, software and programming technique. The uses are as varied as your imagination but the principals and operation are straightforward.

The system starts with a sensor. The sensor is basically a very accurate on/off switch. This sensor is attached to the Z axis of the machine so that it can be moved up and down using the Z axis drive.

By accurate, I mean that it will reliably trip on and off within less than a thousandth of an inch of the same position every time. This requires a sensor that is designed specifically for this purpose. Typical on off switches or position sensors are not nearly accurate enough for this application. This also means that the cost of the sensor is somewhat high but, unfortunately, there is no lower cost substitute.

The more sophisticated sensors will trip not only up and down but side to side. These can be used to measure the edge position of a part as well as its thickness.

To use this sensor requires some programming abilities that are not necessarily available from all current CNC controls. These abilities, however, are critical to this application.

The first capability is the ability to define and set values for variables. In computer programming, variables are names to which you can assign a value. Programs can be written using the names or variables rather than fixed numbers. Each time a program is run, a different value can be assigned to the variable so a slightly different program will result.

The position sensor uses a macro, which is another of these special capabilities. A macro is a short program that performs a specific function. The macro can be called from another program using a program command.

In the case of part thickness sensing, the head is moved over the area to be measured and a macro is called. The macro then lowers the sensor until it contacts the part. It then assigns the position of the Z axis to a variable. By comparing the value of this variable to the Z axis position of the tabletop, the exact thickness of the part can be determined.

In use, this thickness value is generally assigned to another variable. Each time the sensor measures thickness it redefines the same variable. If you need to keep track of the part thickness at several locations, it is necessary to define a variable for each measurement location.

There are several reasons why you might need to measure more than one position on a part. We had one application where a thick wood band was placed around a veneered dining room table top. A shape was machined into the wood band and this shape needed to blend with the top of the veneer within less than five thousandths.

In this application, it was impossible to maintain the thickness of the top anywhere near accurately enough and, even if we could, it was near impossible to locate and secure the top within five thousandths. The only answer was to measure the top of the veneer every six inches or so and use these measurements to create a program that exactly matched the top being cut. In this application it took quite a few points to obtain the necessary accuracy.

Part sensors can be used for an almost endless variety of applications. It can measure the depth of a cut and make adjustments if necessary. It can determine if a part is in place before cutting. It can even measure tool wear by comparing the cuts currently being made to those made earlier. I believe that the ability to automatically measure and use those measurements is a key capability of the furniture fabrication concept.

As I talked about part sensors, I talked about variables and macros. These are both part of an advanced control capability that I also feel is mandatory for furniture fabrication. Thermwood calls this feature the Advanced Function Language.

The Advanced Function Language is a true computer language that can be incorporated into the piece part program. Normally, a CNC part program simply consists of "M" and "G" codes that each tell the machine what function to perform or how far to move. The program is static. If a line of code tells the X axis to move twelve inches, the axis will move twelve inches every time the program is run.

To this static set of instructions, the Advanced Function Language adds a dynamic computer language including the ability to define variables and perform logic. The actual commands used have been made to look quite similar to the Basic programming language. Since most programmers know, and can work with Basic, they already know most of the Advanced Function Language.

Now, instead of telling the axis to move twelve inches, you can tell it to move "length". In this example the word "length" is a variable. Now, each time you run the program you can assign a different value to the variable "length" so each time a different cut is made.

The Advanced Function Language goes well beyond just defining variables. Constants and variables can be used in complex mathematical formulas. Their values can be compared and different actions taken depending on the outcome of that comparison. Special commands exist that allow you to read the position of any machine axis or any machine operating parameter. You can even assign new values to certain basic machine parameters such as acceleration. You can control the display and communication capability as well as full file handling capability.

In short, the Advanced Function Language allows you to exercise full and complete control over the entire operation of the system. Literally, there is almost nothing you can think of that you cannot do with this capability. With this capability, however, comes some danger.

Because you can override the basic machine operating parameters, it is possible to bypass operating safeties and cause the machine to damage itself. Obviously, you need to know what you are doing before playing around in this area. For this reason, the Advanced Function Language should only be used by experienced computer programmers.

Although this is a limitation, the Advanced Function Language is a fairly fundamental computer language and does not require a highly experienced, and very expensive, programmer. It does, however, require someone with some programming background. This is not a good place to first learn computer programming.

The Thermwood SuperControl has another technical feature that, although it sounds like a gimmick, is actually almost a necessity for furniture fabrication. This feature, which we have already talked about, is a "talking control"

One characteristic of furniture fabrication is that programs are both long, by current standards, and they are complex. In many instances, the operator is required to reposition parts during the cycle. Also, each cycle requires the machining of a variety of different parts that each need to be located at a specific position on the fixture at a specific time.

Add to this the fact that only one or two pieces may be produced before changing to another product and you have a fundamental problem. Exactly how does the operator know what to do next?

With the variety and complexity, there is virtually no way that a normal operator can remember every sequence for every part. We could write down the instructions, but locating the proper instruction and reading it each time is not something people will normally do. In most cases they will guess at the next step and mistakes will be made.

The talking control is a simple elegant solution to this problem. The control simply tells the operator what to do next. Elaborate instructions are not necessary. A simple reminder of the next step and perhaps the fixture location is all that is normally needed.

The verbal instructions are actually part of the program. The underlying technology is actually somewhat sophisticated but its use is rather simple.

Using a personal computer, audio files can be recorded and saved. This is done by simply setting up the computer and talking into a microphone, just like recording on a tape recorder. For the talking control to function, audio instructions to the operator are recorded and stored as a series of files, one file for each instruction. These audio files are loaded into the control along with the part program.

Thermwood's Advanced Function Language allows instructions to be added anywhere within a part program to play any of these audio files. When time comes to load fixture one, an audio file instructing the operator to load fixture one can be called by the program and played.

Using the talking control provides a highly efficient means of guiding the operator without requiring him or her to stop what they are doling and either go to the control display or read instructions on a printed form. If the instructions are missed, the next instruction can be placed in the program as a comment so that the operator can refer to the control, but in practice, it requires very little instruction to keep the operator functioning in the proper sequence.

Coordinating audio files with the program requires some experimentation. The audio instructions need to be complete enough to provide the operator with the needed information, but not so detailed that it drones on and he or she tunes it out. In preparing the files, you can assume that the operator understands the various operations and simply provide critical information such as the next part to load, the fixture location to use or how to orient the part for the next operation. It is also important to provide the same information as a comment in the program so that if the operator misses the verbal instructions he can refer to the same instructions printed on the control screen.

Playing the audio files is not quite as simple as it first appears. When this feature was first added to the control, the audio file was executed just like any other instruction. The problem with standard instructions is that the machine executes these instructions sequentially. This means that the machine will stop while the audio file is playing. It will only continue after the current instruction, playing the audio file, is completed.

This can add a significant amount of time to the average cycle. In many cases, it is possible to perform some type of useful work while the operator is performing the necessary tasks. For example, if a tool change is needed, it can be performed while the operator is repositioning a part. It is not recommended or safe to actually perform any type of cutting function while the operator is performing a handling task, however, tool changes, measurement or other non-threatening tasks can be performed.

In order for the machine to perform any other task while the audio file is playing requires that two programs run simultaneously. One program is the audio file playback and the second is the task that is occurring at the same time. To accomplish this, Thermwood doesn't simply play the audio file when the program is called. Instead, it launches a new thread that can execute at the same time as the machine cycle.

Thermwood's SuperControl is multi-tasking. This means that it can execute more than one program, or thread, at a time. In the case of audio file playback, the main program encounters an instruction to play the audio file. It then launches the playback and continues to the next instruction after the playback instruction. This gives the programmer a great deal of freedom in designing the part program.

It is desirable to add a program stop at some point while the audio is playing. The program stop command halts execution of the program until the operator presses the start button. In this way, the operator can signal the machine that the part is properly positioned and he or she is ready for the program to continue.

There are cases, however, where we are not necessarily trying to coordinate the operator and the cycle. For example, in a long running program, the operator may have substantial time to perform assembly or other off-line tasks. Every so often during the cycle, the control could inform the operator of its progress so that he or she would know about how long was remaining before they need to again attend to the machine.

In these cases, it is desirable for the machine to continue machining while the audio file is running.

You should begin to see the power and flexibility that a talking control offers. Once you begin to use this feature, you will wonder how it is possible to operate without a control that talks.

Another technical feature that is becoming more and more important is networking. We all have come in contact with networks today and in many companies they are regarded as the essential communications tool. Network capabilities are essential to furniture fabrication, however, when networks are added to CNC routers a level of confusion develops.

The first thing to realize is that all communications links are not networks. For many years a serial communication port called a DNC link has been part of most CNC controls. Many controls today still have this capability, and in some controls it is the only communications capability.

Exactly what is a DNC link? It is essentially a pair of wires that carries data sequentially. It sends data one bit at a time sequentially until all the information has been sent. An eight bit character requires that eight digits be sent, which are assembled into the character at the receiving end.

In the past, this system has been widely used to move data to and from CNC controls and the system worked fairly well at that time. Programs were relatively small and the need for extensive communications was not present.

Today, however, DNC links are much too limited for modern factory communications. It has two basic limitations. Its most serious deficiency is that it is quite slow by today's standards. Communications demands today require the transfer of huge amounts of data.

In the past, a CNC program might consist of ten or twenty thousand bits of information, referred to as 10K or 20K. Today, programming for a single piece of furniture might require a billion or two billion bits of data. A DNC link that might require a few minutes to transfer 10K or 20K of data might require several hours or days to transfer one or two gigabytes.

The other major shortcoming is that in most cases, transferring data on a DNC link required all system resources. The machine would need to stop while the file transfer was occurring. If it was a large file, the machine might be down for several hours to complete the transfer.

To address the shortcomings of serial communications, computer networks were developed. The network consists of a high speed communication line to which two or more computer devices are attached. Complex networks may consist of hundreds or thousands of devices all connected together. The Internet, which is a highly complex network has tens of millions of devices connected together.

Most factories, however, have their own private networks that connect the various PCs together. In a modern factory and most certainly for furniture fabrication, the CNC machines should also be connected to the network.

Modern networks are orders of magnitude faster than simple serial communications. A file that might require an hour to download over a DNC link can be downloaded in a second or two over a network. So, file transfer, even for very large files, is both practical and convenient. But, file transfer is only part of the value of networking.

Once the CNC control is connected to the network it can be used to send and receive E-mail. Machine operators can freely communicate with scheduling, maintenance or material handling people. Management can send instructions directly to production machine operators. On advanced systems, operators can even search company files to try and solve production or machine problems.

On multi-tasking controls, network communications can occur while the machine is in production. Programmers can send new programs to a machine without the machine operator having to set up or participate. In fact, the machine operator might not even know that the new program has been sent until it is time to run it.

Not all CNC controls allow for multi-tasking and some do not have provisions for network communications. In these cases, it might be possible to add a PC to the control, which can be used for the network communications. This does make file transfer more difficult since, on most of these systems, the local PC must connect to the CNC control using a serial communications port. It does however, even with its limitations, offer some of the communication capabilities that are necessary today.

Once the control exists on a network, it should be possible to view, real time, exactly what the control is doing and where, in the production cycle, it is currently operating. This simple concept of being able to tell at any time the exact status of every production machine has been a goal that has been quite difficult to achieve.

Now that advanced controls can exist on a network, it should be much easier to establish this type of production tracking. To make this easier, Thermwood has added to its control an operations monitoring system that runs in the background.

With this system, the functions that you wish to track are first identified. Then, each time the function occurs, the system writes to a file the function that occurred and the time that it occurred.

For example, you might wish to capture every time a new program is loaded, every time the start button is pressed and every change in the feed speed override control. Once these are defined, any time any of the above functions occur, the function and the time it occurred is written to a separate file. Virtually any control function can be monitored in this fashion.

This data can then be used by retrieving the file data and using it to generate operating reports. The system is quite flexible but does require both analysis and custom programming to function. This was left rather flexible since every company has different requirements.

If your control does not have this capability, it might be possible to use a separate PC connected to the control to provide at least some of this data. The operator could indicate to the PC the current operating program. An output from the control could be used to tell the PC each time the program runs, providing a simple program tracking system.

Regardless of the method used, it is important to be able to view the status of the entire factory on a real-time basis.

The final area where technology is impacting production methods is in maintenance. Once the factory systems are running properly, the single most significant threat is downtime. Provided raw material is available, machine downtime is the single biggest production threat.

CNC routers today are relatively reliable. Years ago, the industrial robot industry was bragging that they enjoyed a 98% uptime. When I ran the calculations to see just what that meant, I realized that our customers would be at war if all we achieved was 98%.

In actual practice a CNC router should achieve well over 99% uptime. We tracked these numbers, as best we could, for several years. We discovered that we could achieve about 99.5% uptime by simply building reliability into the equipment and taking care of problems very quickly. To achieve anything better than that required something we couldn't supply, knowledge on the part of the customer. Customer operating errors or neglect seemed to be the cause of this next increment of downtime.

For many years we attempted to train customers so that they avoided common errors and were able to react quickly to problems they couldn't avoid. While this worked fairly well, today's systems provide much more.

The first step in avoiding downtime is to perform routine preventative maintenance tasks on a timely manner. A machine that is properly maintained and lubricated will generally experience less unplanned downtime than a machine that is neglected.

Arbitrary maintenance and lubrication schedules, however, make this somewhat difficult to do. A production company wants to perform only those maintenance tasks that are absolutely necessary. A machine manufacturer wants to make certain that the machine is properly lubricated and maintained so the two are in conflict from the beginning.

The machine manufacturer doesn't know how hard the machine will be used. Some customers will only use the machine a few hours a week to perform light simple tasks. Others will push the machine limits twenty-four hours a day, seven days a week. For which of these do you set up your lubrication and maintenance schedule.

Most machine manufacturers will establish maintenance schedules for the worst case, thereby making certain that the machine will perform properly in the most difficult of situations.

Generally, customers in these taxing applications will follow recommendations and the machines will generally function reliably. Customers in less demanding applications realize, however, that the factory recommended maintenance schedule is too intense for their simple application. They decide they can safely skip the daily or weekly procedures for a less stringent schedule.

Problem is that there is no less stringent schedule. Skipping the required maintenance becomes common and before long, no maintenance is performed at all. The less demanding application becomes the one with the higher probability of downtime.

You can't blame the machine user for not wanting to perform more lubrication and maintenance than is obviously needed. This is where modern technology can help out.

With a good multi-tasking control, it is possible for the machine to keep track of the exact amount of use for every part of a machine. It can then decide exactly when lubrication and maintenance is required. Not too soon and not too late.

Thermwood has offered this capability for several years as part of its Service Guide System. It tracks actual machine use and alerts the operator when routine service is required. It also keeps track of how much time elapses from the time it first notifies the operator until the required maintenance is actually performed.

The Service Guide System goes one step farther. When maintenance is actually performed, it shows a detailed three dimensional drawing of the machine areas to maintain and provides step by step directions to the maintenance people. This insures that some part of the maintenance procedure is not inadvertently missed, which is another common cause of machine problems.

This approach offers the advantage of not requiring too much maintenance on intermittent, light duty applications while insuring that the necessary preventative maintenance is performed so that machine problems can be avoided.

Another area where technology can help reduce downtime is when a problem does occur. A lot of time can be wasted after a problem occurs, simply trying to identify the problem. A lot of controls use cryptic codes for errors. To decode these usually requires the manual, which was likely lost long ago. Eventually a call to the service department leads to identification of a problem that might be a simple blown fuse.

With modern technology, it is also possible to not only identify the problem but offer useful solutions. On Thermwood's control, an error signal automatically brings up a three-dimensional drawing of the machine with a list of possible causes for the error and arrows showing, where to check. This can save countless hours of frustration and allows simple errors to be found and corrected fast enough that they have little or no impact on production.

One other area that I feel is extremely important is labeling. Many CNC controls rely on wire color or numbers to identify electrical components in the control. You might discover that the problem is a blown fuse, but then require an electrical drawing and a half an hour to locate the fuse inside the control.

I believe that every major electrical component in the control cabinet should be labeled with its function, in English. It should be possible to locate every major part without referring to a diagram, schematic or manual. This simple, inexpensive step can save hours of maintenance time when a problem does occur. If your machine or control supplier hasn't performed this task, it is worth your while to have your maintenance people take the time to identify and label these components yourself.

We have now covered the major technology that is part of Furniture Fabrication, one at a time. We will now see how all these individual technologies work together to make a modern Furniture Fabrication Factory.

# Chapter 6

## Running the Factory

# Chapter 6

## Running the factory

At this point, we will examine the actual operation of a furniture fabrication factory. Describing the actual operation should answer many questions that might otherwise require detailed explanations. We will not only look at normal every day operation, but we will also examine the effect of problems and disruptions on the operation. When we look at the effect of these problems, try and imagine the effect of the same problem on your factory.

To describe the operation of the factory we will need to create an imaginary furniture fabrication factory. We will use a typical casegoods layout as we described earlier in this book for this exercise.

It is in the ability of this factory structure to easily handle problems and situations that give it a major advantage over a conventional factory. Most managers analyze a factory structure by examining only the production process operating properly. There are two problems with this approach.

First, production processes do not operate properly all the time. The structure in which disruptions have the least negative effect is obviously superior to a structure that requires perfection to be productive.

The second problem is that most factory structures have many, many productivity leeches. These leeches are not major problems themselves, but they each suck a little productivity from the operation. When combined with hundreds of other leeches, they can turn a highly productive plan into a marginal operation.

These productivity leeches are the major reason that the productivity and performance projected by the engineering plan are seldom reached in practice. Your accounting system has no way of tracking these productivity leeches. There is also very little chance of identifying and correcting all these problems. Each is small and simple enough that it is almost insignificant in itself. Any productivity leech that is identified can be corrected. The real problem is in identifying them all, and their large numbers.

I almost hate to give specific examples of productivity leeches because they come in so many sizes and variations. If I focus you on a few examples you may very well ignore a multitude of them that do not fit the example. Nonetheless, they include things like disposing of packing materials, trying to handle parts with gloves, congested areas that slow material handling, poorly lighted areas that make part identification difficult, scrap pieces that jam conveyors, chunks that wedge in the dust collection system, cracks in the floor that make pallet trucks difficult to move, areas that are difficult to sweep up, doors that are difficult to open or close, blind spots that require fork trucks to slow down. There are thousands of these in every factory. The larger and more complex the factory, the more productivity leeches there are.

And, therein lies the answer. It is not common for leeches to live within a machine itself. Machine manufacturers spend considerable effort to make their product as effective as possible. If your machine supplier has been in business any time at all, they have likely eliminated these little problems. Productivity leeches live between production centers and in the material handling process. The simpler the factory structure and the simpler the material flow, the fewer areas in which productivity leeches can exist. By their very nature, they require a complex factory to live. If you can develop a simple structure with little material handling and few machines, productivity leeches will have few places to live. This is even true if the few machines are somewhat sophisticated and complex.

The reason that I addressed this area now, is that as we describe the operation of a furniture fabrication factory, the basic operation will look quite simple. What you won't see is that the advantage is even greater than it appears on the surface. Not only is the structure simple and straightforward, but there is little breeding ground for productivity leeches. If designed properly, this structure operates very close to the theoretical model.

In our imaginary factory we will build medium to high-end case goods. We will focus on chests, dressers and nightstands. These will be built from veneer covered plywood panels and hardwood face frames, doors and drawers. We will offer several period styles from simple country to carved French provincial. To add some additional interest, we will allow for variations of each style.

By variations, we mean that the species of wood as well as the shapes used on the doors, drawers and top can be selected by the customer. We can also allow a selection of finish and hardware.

This idea of allowing the customer to select a random combination of product features is called mass customization. There is a general feeling that mass customization will become part of the future of manufacturing simply because modern computer systems make this both possible and practical. With this change, the furniture industry will be forced to offer mass customization in order to compete.

Recently I have heard some knowledgeable people predict that within a few years, mass produced items will take on the character of being somewhat cheap and inferior. Unless the item is somewhat customized for each customer, it will be considered undesirable and perhaps unacceptable.

If you think about it, it is more difficult to offer mass customization from a foreign manufacturing facility. The distribution chain is too long to be practical. Therefore, if US based furniture manufacturers offer mass customization with no price penalty, they should enjoy a competitive advantage. This very well could be the difference between keeping the market and losing it to foreign competition.

As you will see, building furniture that is mass customizeded is no more difficult than building the exact same piece each time. In fact, the cell operator does not even need to know what custom features were selected. The system makes all the changes automatically, selecting the proper tool shapes as necessary. We will talk about mass customization in more detail later in this book.

Although we have selected casegoods for our example, most of the operations and techniques also apply to other types of furniture. Casegoods offer a combination of hardwood machining techniques plus nested based panel manufacturing so it seemed like a good choice for this example.

Material is trucked into the loading dock area. It is bundled in material kits. Dresser kits contain the material needed for one dresser except for the veneer covered panels and the face frame stock. These materials are stored as common stock at each cell. The dresser kits include blanks for the doors and drawer fronts, the drawer components and the base. Dresser kits are packaged ten to skid, only because it is a convenient skid height and amounts to about one shift's worth of production for a cell. Chests and nightstands are packaged with a different number of pieces per skid.

The actual packaging of the material kits should be analyzed to make the production process as smooth as possible. Those parts that are used first in the cycle should be packaged on top and those parts used later should be below. As a general rule, the operator should be able to pick the parts off the skid in the order in which they are used. This practice makes the production process smoother and makes the possibility of selecting the wrong blank less likely.

The skids are unloaded at the truck dock and moved to a storage rack. A warehouseman controls material within the storage area, either by himself or working with a fork truck driver. The skids of material are moved to locations within the storage area where the identity and location of each skid of material is input into the material handling computer database.

The most accurate way to accomplish this is by using bar code readers. The identity of the material is scanned in using the bar code reader. The quantity and location are then added providing a complete, up to the minute status of the entire raw material inventory area.

There are a variety of systems available for tracking inventory. Some of these are quite sophisticated using radio frequency to transmit data from the fork truck to the control computer. Others use identification tags that tell the computer what they are and where they are.

Many of the systems available today are intended to help control the complex material flow through current furniture factories. Only a tiny fraction of their capabilities are needed to track and control inventory through a simple furniture fabrication factory.

I am not going to go into the design and operation of these systems in depth. This technology is changing fast and I believe that as furniture fabrication becomes more accepted, systems will become available that fit the requirements better.

The storage racks are about fifteen feet high and allow skids to be stored one high on shelves. Each shelf location is labeled with a location number. The actual number of kits stored on a skid is generally determined by the overall height of the package. This overall height is determined by the spacing between storage shelves. Skid height is kept to a level that allows easy storage and retrieval without wasting space.

The primary task of the warehouseman is to make certain that the inventory database is accurate. This includes both raw material and finished goods. The warehouseman is also responsible for shipping out finished goods and tracking shipment data.

Once these tasks are complete, he or she can then assist the cell operators with individual material handling tasks.

Let us begin the manufacture of a dresser. We received a work order to build a dresser. On this work order is a bar code that defines what we are to build. Scan the bar code using the scanner on the CNC router control.

The correct program for the dresser is now loaded into the machine control. The first line of the new program tells you to load fixture number 123.

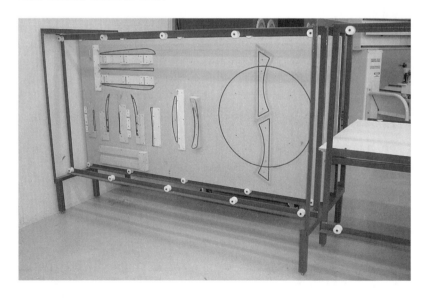

The fixture handling cart is moved to the fixture storage area. In this area, fixtures are stored on edge in a rack. The distance between fixtures is the same as the clearance under the machine tooling so that any fixture than will work in the machine will also store in the rack.

The fixture handling cart has two tilt racks that can be positioned either horizontally or vertically. A fixture fits into each rack. The fixture is rolled from the storage rack into the handling cart while in the vertical orientation.

The fixture rack and new fixture is rolled to the machine. A foot operated brake secures the cart so it will not easily move. Vacuum, holding the old fixture is turned off and the old fixture is slid off the machine and onto the handling cart. A lift button at the front of the machine table aids in lifting the old fixture from inside the machine table.

The old fixture is slid off the machine and onto the fixture handling cart.

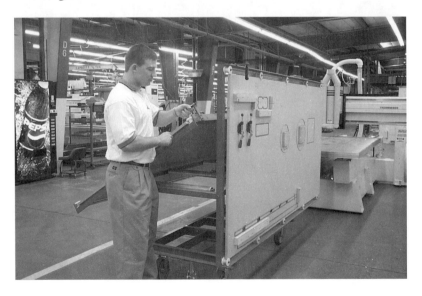

The old fixture is now rotated to the vertical position.

The new fixture is rotated to the horizontal position.

The new fixture is then slid into the machine table.

Once the new fixture is slipped into the table, vacuum is turned on and the fixture change is complete. This entire process only takes a few minutes and can be accomplished by one person.

We now press the start button on the machine. In a voice, broadcast through the system speakers, it asks you to scan the fixture. Using the bar code reader you scan the bar code on the fixture you just loaded. The system makes certain that you loaded the correct fixture for this piece.

If the bar codes don't match, the control notifies you that a mismatch exists and will not run the program until the CNC program and the fixture properly match. This virtually eliminates machine crashes, which are a major cause of machine damage and downtime.

You now press the start button again and the machine head moves to the left where it unloads the tools currently in the automatic tool changer connected to the head. These tools are automatically placed into a bulk tool changer. The bulk tool changer can hold up to fifty different tools. Then the system scans the new program to determine which tools will be needed. It then retrieves those tools from the bulk tool changer, placing them in the appropriate positions in the tool changer at the head.

Perhaps the tooling manager has replaced some of the older used tools with new sharp tools. For each of these, the system will automatically move to a tool length sensor and will measure the exact length of the new tool. This length is automatically entered in to the tool table of the machine. All programs that use this new tool length will now be automatically adjusted for the new tool length.

Since the tools are used randomly for different parts, how does the tooling manager know when a tool is becoming dull? It is virtually impossible to keep track of tool life manually. Generally, the cell operator will only notice that a tool isn't performing properly when it begins producing scrap parts. That is too late. The disruptions to the production process represent a serious increase in cost even without considering the cost of the scrapped material.

It is also not practical to try and manually check each tool on a schedule. With fifty to a hundred tools per cell, and potentially many cells in the factory, the job of checking tools manually is just not reasonable. Instead, an estimated life for each tool is determined. This life is entered into the tool management system, which is part of the machine control. As the tool is used to cut, the actual cutting time is automatically subtracted from the estimated life. When the life becomes zero, a warning message is posted on the control.

If the factory processes different materials using the same tooling and if these materials have differing tool wear properties, the system must be modified. For example a tool cutting a soft material such as pine might last much longer than the same tool cutting a difficult material such as hickory. If both materials will be cut in the same cell, a single tool life value will not work.

In these cases, an average tool life value can be modified by the program. A command within the program can instruct the control to reduce tool life at a faster or slower rate depending on the material being cut. For example, if the program is going to cut a material that wears tools out twice as fast, the command will instruct the control to subtract tool life twice as fast. In this way, tool sharpness can be estimated rather accurately after a little experience.

CNC controls for all cells are networked together. The tooling manager also has a computer on the network and can access the tooling data for each cell. From the tooling list, he or she can determine which tools have either expired or are about to expire and can change those tools before they begin producing scrap.

If a production run is long and tooling life for a particular tool is short, it is possible to have more than one copy of the same tool loaded in the bulk tool changer. As one tool is used up, the machine automatically switches to the second, sharp tool. This offers the tooling manager more time to service and replace the dull tools without the cell waiting for tooling service.

These features and capabilities are not a wish list for the future. As this book is being written, all the tooling management features I have just described exist and most are available as standard products. Also, without these features, tool management can become a real stumbling block to getting full productivity from a furniture fabrication cell.

Now we are ready. The new program is loaded, the new fixture is mounted, verified and ready and the proper tooling is loaded and ready.

It is interesting to note that all this was done without the cell operator needing to know the technical details of the new program. The cell operator made no adjustments for size. He did not need to know the diameter, description or location for any tool. The system took care of the technical details of changing from one part to the next.

There are several advantages to this approach. First, it requires much less time. If you watch a traditional change over cycle, you will find that well over half of the time required is used trying to determine what to do and how to do it. Measurements are calculated, checked and re-checked. In many companies, the first parts off the new setup must be verified by QC. This requires not only an extra step, but possibly a wait while the QC inspector handles the parts that came in before you.

Automatic setup reduces or eliminates errors. Regardless of how careful you are, the traditional approach will eventually result in an expensive mistake because it relies on human judgment.

Automatic setup is digital, occurs with little human intervention and seldom, if ever, results in an error that is not caught by the system.

Finally, a less technically skilled cell operator can perform automatic setup. Employees with the skill level needed to perform complex changeovers on traditional machines are becoming more difficult to find. In general, they are able to find more challenging, better paying jobs than changing your machine from part to part, over and over again.

We are ready to run. Press start again and the control tells you what to do. In an audio voice, it directs you to place certain materials into certain fixtures on the table. Simply follow directions and build a piece of furniture.

The audio output, at first, seems like a gimmick rather than a real necessity. In fact, it is much easier to listen to the instructions than to stop what you are doing, go to the control screen, find the instructions on the screen, read them and interpret them. In fact, without the audio instructions, you would likely not read every instruction. This is especially true after you have built a few of the piece you are currently working on.

As you change from piece to piece, eventually you will make a mistake relying solely on memory. The audio files provide that little extra guidance to keep you on track.

If the manufacturing process is properly designed, you will be performing certain machining functions off the machine. For example, you will use a simple manual dovetailing machine to cut the dovetails in the drawer body. Although this function can be performed on the machine, it uses valuable cycle time.

How do you determine whether a function should be performed on the CNC machine or on a manual machine off-line? This is a judgment call based on several factors.

First is setup. You should not use any secondary machine that requires setup. The only machines that should be used for secondary operations are those that are always set for the function required. A drawer dovetailer, for example, can be used to quickly dovetail a drawer side and does not need to be changed for different sized drawers.

Should you only require a couple of different setups, it might make sense to have two different machines, one set up for the first part and one set up for the second.

Do not succumb to the temptation to substitute a simple setup for a whole new piece of equipment. As soon as you add setup, even a tiny setup you destroy the flow and advantages of this system. A more qualified cell operator is needed, a decision needs to be made and setup information must be communicated. Before long, the cell will deteriorate into traditional manufacturing with all its limitations and problems.

The second thing that determines if secondary operations make sense is the cost of the machine needed to perform those operations.

If it is a fairly low cost simple machine, it might make sense to do the job off line. If the machine is either expensive or complex it is generally better to perform the task on the main cell CNC machine. We are trying to maximize the production and minimize the capital expenditure. If a low cost machine can materially reduce machining time on a high cost CNC router and it does not require setup, it likely makes sense. On the other hand, if the secondary machine is high cost, requires setup and does not markedly reduce cycle time on the cell, it should be avoided.

This can be seen with the drawer dovetails. If the dovetails are done on the CNC router, the drawer side must be mounted on a vertical table. The dovetails are then machined one at a time using the router. This takes substantially longer than placing the drawer side into manual dovetailer and pressing a button.

Even this rule isn't always the case, however. For a trade show we built a reproduction of a Newport kneehole bureau. This was a solid walnut piece that was first built by hand in the late 1700s. To achieve an accurate reproduction we wanted to produce dovetails that looked "hand made". To achieve this goal, we decided to vary the width of each dovetail with no two being exactly the same. This is virtually impossible to do on a traditional dovetailing machine and so the dovetails were cut on the CNC router even though it was slower.

Also, some manual dovetailers use the diameter of the dovetail bit to set the size of the resulting dovetail. This can lead to assembly problems if the size varies from the standard. More sophisticated CNC dovetailers use toll radius compensation to allow for variations in cutter diameter but these are quite a bit more expensive and the additional cost may not be justified.

Another factor that determines whether a secondary operation makes sense is accuracy. If tolerances for the secondary operations are tight and difficult to achieve, the process should be performed on the CNC machine. If, however, tolerances are loose or non-existent or are easy to achieve, the process may lend itself to secondary operations.

Do not perform so many secondary operations that either the operator doesn't have time to assemble or that the CNC machine is waiting on the secondary operations.

As you can see, determining if something should be done as a secondary operation requires judgment. There is no right answer and there are no fixed rules. You should do whatever seems to make the most sense keeping in mind the overall philosophy and goals for the cell.

If the cell and programming was set up properly, you can load, unload and assemble the dresser quite easily in the time available. There should be enough extra time to keep the work area clean and to move materials in and out of the cell area.

You assemble the dresser using a four wheel cart. The base is placed on the cart and then the various components are assembled on the base. When complete, the cart is rolled to the center quality inspection area. When the dresser is approved for finishing, the cart is rolled to a moving floor conveyor and the front of the cart is attached to the conveyor chain. The conveyor moves the cart from the cell production area to the finishing room.

Designing and running the cell may require a rethinking of some basic manufacturing processes. By their very nature, some processes require large, specialized and expensive equipment. This type of process cannot be performed in a cell arrangement.

To accommodate this type of process, the process itself must be moved back into the rough fabrication area where it can be operated in a high volume mode. To understand this better, let us use a common example.

Dressers, desks and other types of casegoods commonly use tops that are a combination of a particleboard or plywood core, edge banded with a hardwood frame and covered with a wood veneer. The normal process for this top is to first cut the core material to size. Then the four hardwood edges are attached to the core and the panel is sanded to assure that the hardwood bands and the core are even. Then a veneer cover is bonded to the panel and finally the edge of the panel is shaped to the final contour.

This process isn't going to work very well in a fabrication cell for several reasons. A belt sander wide enough to sand the entire top will not fit the cell very well and a veneer press certainly won't work in the cell. In general, the whole process doesn't lend itself to cell manufacturing very well.

You could produce the tops off-line at a separate top area but this eliminates some of the benefits of nested based manufacturing and begins to turn our new, modern factory back into a traditional furniture plant. We need to approach the problem from another direction.

While the look and construction of the top is more or less fixed, the method of achieving that result is not fixed. Let us produce the same top but using the strengths of the CNC router rather than expensive, specialized equipment.

Instead of starting with a plain piece of particleboard or plywood, we will start with a veneer covered panel. The veneering process has now been moved back into the rough mill where it can be performed efficiently, in volume, at low cost.

Next, the top is cut as part of a nest in a nested based operation. The parts are all removed from the table and the top is flipped so that the veneered face is lying flat on the vacuum tabletop. Next, the edge of the panel is machined through the core material but not through the veneer. A mortise slot is also cut into the edge of the panel.

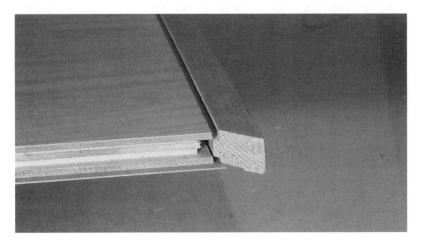

A hardwood edge band is inserted into the machined panel edge to support the veneer and provide the material into which the edge shape can be cut.

The exposed veneer edge on the panel will be somewhat fragile. It is best if it is handled as little as possible until the hardwood edge is inserted. The best approach is to cut the edges first, then glue and insert them into the machined top panel right after machining while it is still held in place on the machine table. This does tie up the machine during the assembly process but should result in much less scrap and fewer edge breakage problems.

The final result of this operation is a top that is essentially identical to tops produced the conventional way. The difference is that this top can be efficiently produced in the cell. It will usually be less expensive since the somewhat higher cost of the veneered panels is normally much less than the labor, material handling and extra equipment required in the traditional approach.

This is just one example of the type of thinking that is necessary to make furniture fabrication actually work. This is a new technology and to make this new technology work will require new thinking. This new thinking is not easy.

The way things are done today is strongly ingrained in the wood industry. This rigid thinking is very hard to break, even when you really want to change it. The only advice I can offer is to start with the basic concept of the fabrication cell. We want to machine and assemble the entire piece of furniture in a cell. Anything that prevents this needs to be revised, even if it is the accepted industry practice. If you approach the problems with this view, you will find that furniture fabrication will work very well in your factory.

Now let's look at some typical problems. First, I need a rush shipment now.

This is really not a problem for furniture fabrication at all. Simply load the pieces needed as the next products to build for one or several cells, and in an hour or two, the assembled pieces are ready to finish. Even if we are only talking about one or two pieces, they can be built and ready to finish in a couple of hours at most.

Now consider the same problem for a traditional factory. If you are lucky, the pieces you need can be found in your huge finished goods warehouse or can be stolen from another order. If you need to build the pieces, you are in real trouble.

Entire skids of material for each and every component of the piece must be located. Every machine that every component goes through must be set up and the component machined and then checked. All these parts must be moved to the assembly department where the piece is finally assembled. Or perhaps, you have a sample shop that can make the pieces and handle the problem. In general, however, this type of problem is simply not handled because the cost of actually building just one or two pieces is just too high.

Lets look at another typical problem. You are operating under a just-in-time inventory system and it just-didn't-make-it. The material you need for the top of the five drawer chest didn't show up and you need the parts to complete the run and assemble the chests. Everything else showed up and has been processed, but the tops are just not here. Let's look at the impact.

We can start building the next cutting, but it won't be ready to assemble until late tomorrow. The finishing line, which was supposed to be finishing the five drawer chests doesn't have anything to finish. The assembly department also doesn't have anything to assemble. Luckily, the next cutting will be ready for assembly tomorrow morning, but so will the five drawer chest. The parts finally showed up. Tomorrow, the assembly department and the finishing department who don't have anything to do today, will have too much to do tomorrow.

Let's look at the same problem in a furniture fabrication factory. Now, the parts that didn't show up are not the top or the side, it is everything. Because we receive raw material in material kits, when a shipment doesn't show up on time, everything doesn't show up on time.

Even though this seems like a bigger problem, it isn't. If none of the materials required show up, there is no temptation to start processing some of the parts. Much of the confusion is gone. The fabrication cells simply process anything on order for which material kits do exist. These pieces are certainly being built out of sequence, but everyone is busy and the flow of product to the finishing room is steady and uninterrupted. When the material for the five drawer chest does show up, you simply switch back to five drawer chests at the next cycle and the overall impact is minimal.

In this case, a problem that is devastating to both throughput and organization in a traditional furniture factory is a non-event that can be recovered from in less than a day in a furniture fabrication factory.

Now, let's look at some processing problems. Lets start with a broken machine. Although today's machines are highly reliable, they are not perfect. This same thing goes for older, more traditional woodworking machines. If it moves, every so often it will break.

Let's start with a traditional furniture factory and assume that one of the primary processing machines, a double end tenoner, for example, breaks. In each case let us assume we need a replacement part and we can get it overnight.

Now, every part that was supposed to go through this machine can't. Other parts are going through other machines but furniture can't be assembled and a hole exists in the production flow. If you are lucky, you have enough in-process material to keep things going until the part is received, the machine fixed and perhaps some overtime and things are back in sync. If the machine is down long enough to run out of in-process, disruptions occur.

Many furniture companies operate with substantial inventories of material between production centers for just such a problem. This is very expensive although it does offer a little cushion. If the machine is down for any extended period of time, however, the cushion will eventually disappear. Once this occurs, the problems described above start to occur.

This is a good case for "backup" machines. If you are large enough, you can have several double end tenoners. If one goes down, overtime on the others keep things going until the problem is fixed. This is an advantage for furniture fabrication as well.

If a fabrication cell goes down, all production for that cell stops. All other cells, however, keep producing finished furniture. One cell does not depend on the other. If you have five cells running and one goes down, simply run the other four cells two hours overtime and the overall production is the same.

What about improperly sized parts? With a fabrication cell, part sizing is a function of the machine. In most cases, if the machine is operating, the resulting parts will be the correct size.

With traditional woodworking, size adjustments are analog. An operator or set-up technician turns a screw that adjusts the position of the cutter and determines the size of the resulting part. Since mistakes at this level can and do occur, generally a quality inspection and approval is required before processing the remainder of the batch.

With these checks and experience, mistakes happen very seldom, but they do happen. When an error does occur, the entire cutting is cut the wrong size. If it was cut too large, it simply needs to be cut again. If it was cut too small, it will still be too small even if you cut it off again.

If scrap is cut in traditional manufacturing generally the entire batch is scrapped.

The impact of a scrapped batch is similar to the impact of late material or machine problems. If you can remake the batch quickly and you have enough in-process inventory, the impact can be mild. If you do not, the impact can be expensive.

Although mis-sized parts are difficult to produce on a CNC machine, let us assume that somehow this does occur. Perhaps we made a programming error or used the wrong material. In any case, the impact is minimal. Since we assemble every piece as we cut it, as soon as we try and assemble the piece, we will discover the error. The result is one scrapped part, or perhaps even a scrapped piece of furniture. It is virtually impossible to scrap an entire batch since batch processing doesn't exist.

Furniture fabrication, however, does have a problem that doesn't exist in traditional manufacturing. That problem is scrapping a single part. In furniture fabrication, it is possible to scrap a part because of flaws in the raw materials. For example, you could receive veneered 4 x 8 sheets in which flaws exist in the veneer. When these sheets are cut into components, some of the components may be unusable. Only one or two parts may be scrapped from each sheet, but this does cause a disruption since the finished piece of furniture cannot be assembled without these pieces.

It is also possible to run a scrap hardwood piece in furniture fabrication. Hardwoods may have internal faults, knots or split grain that result in an unusable part. Recovery from these types of problems depend on whether the scrapped parts are panels or hardwood components.

Let's start with recovery from a defective panel. The first thing to realize is that panel stock is not part of the material kit for the piece. Therefore, the replacement part or parts will need to be cut from the general panel stock.

The most obvious approach is to simply re-cut the entire nest that contains the defective part. This will provide you with not only a replacement part, but also extra parts from the nest. If, because of material problems or other reasons, it is somewhat common to scrap panel parts, this approach might make sense. The extra parts might very well be used to replace other scrapped parts.

If, however, it is not common to scrap panel parts, then this approach will result in the production and storage of many extra parts that will likely never be used. In this case, we need to use a different approach.

Thermwood is currently working on a system that operates at the machine to make replacement parts. This system can retrieve any part from the nested program and translate it to a fixed locator fence.

To use this system, you hand cut a blank slightly oversized and locate it using the locator fence. The replacement part is selected and the machine cuts a replacement piece. It is likely that by the time you read this, this system will be a standard part of our package.

Other companies use CAM systems to nest and create the programs. These CAM systems are also able to create individual part programs. If scrapped parts are a common problem, these individual part programs could be generated and downloaded with little extra effort providing the operator with an easy way to generate replacements.

These approaches are very effective if you scrap only a single part and this happens very infrequently. Another possibility is that a single batch of material causes problems. In this case, you are faced with replacing several parts.

You can simply hand cut blanks and process the needed parts one at a time, but this approach will generally result in poor material yield. You will not be able to manually nest the blanks very efficiently.

In this case, it is possible to go back to the program that first created the nest. In the design section, turn off all parts except the ones required as replacements. Then re-nest the remaining pieces. This will result in a program in which only the replacement parts are nested on full sheets of material.

Although this process sounds complex, it is actually quite simple. The entire effort can be accomplished by an experienced person in ten to fifteen minutes. The resulting program is then networked to the machine and run. This could very well take less time than hand cutting the blanks needed for one at a time replacement machining.

If parts from the material kits are scrapped, it will be necessary to get another blank from a new material kit. This leaves a kit with a missing part. There are several methods of addressing this.

One approach is to establish a broken kit area. In this area, material kits with missing parts are stored. If a replacement part is needed, the cell operator first checks the broken kit area to see if a replacement part is available. If not, then the part must be taken from a complete kit and the remaining materials taken to the broken kit area.

If the number of broken kits increases, it is possible to selectively add the missing parts to the broken kits and return them to raw material stock.

With reasonable quality materials and a good tooling program, it should be very seldom that parts are scrapped in furniture fabrication. Should it happen, however, methods need to be established to quickly recover.

Overall, it appears to be much easier to plan, operate and handle problem situations in furniture fabrication than with more traditional furniture manufacturing.

As this book is being written, my company has just begun shipping integrated kitchen cabinet manufacturing packages. These systems are very similar to furniture fabrication, except that every product produced is custom. After only a couple of week's experience, one of these new customers has started a second shift. He explained to us "There are so few things that can go wrong with this system that a second shift makes perfect sense".

I believe that this same thing will apply to building furniture using essentially the same techniques.

# Chapter 7

## Mass Customization

# Chapter 7

## Mass Customization

I believe that this chapter will introduce concepts that will make most furniture manufacturers very uncomfortable. I also believe that these ideas hold the key to survival for furniture manufacturing in the United States.

The reason that mass customization strikes fear into furniture manufacturing executives is that the present manufacturing methods cannot possibly deal with the requirements. If the industry embraces these ideas, it will have to totally change the way its product is built. What exactly is mass customization?

Mass customization is mass producing a product but customizing every one of these products for the individual customer. It doesn't mean offering several variations that the customer can choose from. Instead it means allowing the customer to actually provide design input and then using that design input to build a product specifically for that customer. Generally the number of variations is large enough that you cannot build standard products and then select from inventory when a customer orders a product. Instead, the product must generally be built for a particular customer to his or her specifications.

Today, a customer can go to a custom furniture builder and have virtually anything built. These companies exist and, for a price, they will custom build anything you want. If however, you don't want to pay the high custom price, you are forced to choose from furniture pieces that are being offered by the major mass builders of furniture. Prices are much less but selection is more limited.

Technology is about to change this.

The idea of mass customization is taking hold in the US. This means, without paying the high price for a completely custom product, the consumer can still have a product customized for their needs or wants. In addition, these custom products can be obtained in a relatively short period of time.

These ideas are already becoming available for many products. Recently I saw an ad where a well known maker of tennis shoes were willing to custom make special shoes, with custom color combinations and a monogram for only a small additional charge over their normal retail price. The lead time was only a few weeks and the premium was $10.

If you think about this offer, however, you realize that it can be a very profitable item for the manufacturer. These custom shoes are being offered over the Internet. As a factory direct sale, not only is the manufacturer getting the $10 premium but they are also getting the retail markup. In fact, the manufacturer is likely getting over twice the normal price for each pair of shoes.

These same ideas are taking hold in other areas including automobiles, clothing and I believe, furniture.

This idea may offer a way to effectively compete with low cost foreign labor. One of the basic problems with foreign production of furniture is the long supply chain. It would be difficult to build custom furniture for a customer order and then ship it across the world. Eve if it could be done at a competitive price, the time requirement should put the foreign manufacturer at a competitive disadvantage. Low cost foreign suppliers rely on volume production and shipment for their cost advantage. They also focus on products where low cost labor is the determining factor.

Mass customization depends more on advanced technology then on low cost labor. It should be possible to offer customized products from within the United States to customers within the US and enjoy a competitive advantage.

Customized furniture may also provide a method whereby the furniture industry can begin selling direct, over the web without destroying their current distribution system. Standard pieces could be sold through normal distribution. Customized pieces could be sold, at a slight premium, over the Internet. The Internet sales should, in fact, be extremely profitable.

This approach could also provide an avenue for established furniture companies to begin adopting furniture fabrication methods. The large majority of furniture could continue to be built using current factories and sold through traditional distribution. Customized furniture could be sold on the web and built using fabrication cells. As web sales increase in proportion to traditional sales, production facilities could be switched over.

In this chapter I want to examine this idea of mass customization as it pertains to furniture manufacturing. I would like to look at the practical aspects of actually doing this on an ongoing basis. Some customization is easy while others may be quite difficult. I will discuss the areas that furniture fabrication makes easy. There very well could be additional areas that develop in the future, however, I will focus on the technology that currently exists and discuss how this might be used to offer a form of customization to the customer.

First, let us look at those areas that can be customized on a piece of furniture. The first thing that mass customization does is present the furniture designer with a much more difficult task. Each piece of furniture and each available custom feature must blend together so that any final result at least looks presentable. To some extent we must protect the customer from designing a completely awful final product.

This design problem could become a major stumbling block. Most furniture designers I have worked with have very strong and definite ideas of what is right and wrong. There is little room for modifying what they believe is a perfect design.

To offer mass customization, the furniture designer must be willing to offer both a perfect design as well as allowing other people to modify the design to their own liking even if the result is less than perfect. To accomplish this will require, at least, different thinking on the part of the furniture designer. It may require a different type of furniture designer altogether.

At this point, the furniture designer will need to make certain that overall proportions of each piece of furniture are appropriate. They will need to choose edge profiles that will all work together and will need to make certain that finishes and hardware can be combined without major problems.

Let us look at different aspects of case goods to determine those areas that can be customized within the furniture fabrication system.

First, the basic type of furniture can be determined. Is it a six drawer chest, a dresser, a nightstand or a desk? Here, I believe the customer should select from pre-determined types of furniture. It makes no sense to try and create a universal case good piece and then modify it to a desk or dresser.

In fact, I believe that the best design for each piece, from the designers standpoint, should be offered and displayed and then the customization points offered. We will use this approach.

Let's start with a dresser. We can start with the size. I, for one, do not believe that it is necessary to offer basic size variations for customized furniture. Nonetheless, from a technical standpoint, producing different sized pieces is technically possible today. For hardwood products, material cost for all sized pieces will be equal to the material cost for the largest piece, since material kits need to accommodate the largest possible piece. These materials will then be cut down for the smaller pieces.

For products made from panel stock and hardwood, smaller parts could result in slightly lower material cost since the exact parts specified will be computer nested. Yield will change dynamically in this type of operation.

There are several ways to accommodate custom sized furniture pieces. The first is to generate individual sets of part programs for each size offered. Creating a set of programs using modern design software is relatively fast and easy. All the different programs could be combined into one large program. Variables input through a bar code could then select the appropriate sub routines to run.

From the cell operator's standpoint, all he or she needs to do is scan the bar code or load the next program from the network and follow the audio directions. The parts are cut and, when assembled, produce the desired size finished piece. From a practical standpoint, it is no more difficult to make a custom size than to make a standard size.

Another approach is to feed the new sizes into a design software package and then custom generate programs for the new piece. Although this will offer little benefit when cutting the hardwood parts, it could offer slightly better nesting and yield when cutting smaller pieces from full sheets of material.

For a particular batch, a number of different pieces of furniture can be selected. The overall size of each piece selected can also be specified. At this point, the computer system creates programs for the individual parts and nests them on the sheet material. This should offer much better material yield than is possible using unique individual programs.

This is essentially how custom sized kitchen cabinets are made in nested based manufacturing. The cabinets are designed on a computer screen. They are modified until the customer is totally happy with the final result. Then, the programs necessary to build the cabinets are generated and downloaded to the machine where they are cut. Once the design is complete, it only takes a few seconds to generate the programs and download them.

Another alternative is to create the programs used to make the different pieces using variables instead of fixed dimensions. For example, the height, width and depth of the piece could be the variables. Then, the programs for all the parts are written using the variables. When time comes to cut the parts, all the operator must do is input the height, width and depth, by scanning a bar code, and all the parts will be cut to make a piece of the proper size.

Although this technology is currently available, writing these parametric programs is currently a somewhat tedious task. For this reason, to date, this system has only been used for relatively simple parts such as cabinet doors.

As you can see, offering custom sizes is technically feasible even though I am not certain that it will be required for this market to be successful.

After size, the next thing that can be customized are the design features. The most common design features of a piece of furniture are the edge shapes of the various components. The profile edge of the drawers, doors and top have a major influence on the overall look of the piece. Changing these design features is actually quite simple. These edge profiles are determined by the profile of the tool used to cut the edge. By simply using a different tool, it is possible to customize the design of the piece.

In this case, the actual programs are the same. The only difference is that in one instance the program is run with one tool and in the next it is run with a different tool. Furniture fabrication can easily accommodate this requirement.

Again, we will use variables. Here the variables will indicate the tools to use. At the beginning of the program, the variables are defined either using a bar code or network input. When the program is run, the desired tools are used to cut the various profiles. The result is a customized piece, although the operator is running exactly the same program.

Other design features such as carvings on the face or on the side rails can be customized in the same fashion.

In each of these cases, with very little disruption to the operator, customized pieces have been produced. Even more important, the cell operator does not need to determine or know what to customize. The customization just happens.

This same basic technique can be used to offer almost any level of customization. Carving programs can be selected using bar codes and macros to provide some real custom choices.

In addition to the basic changes in the cutting and detailing of the components, other custom changes can also be accomplished easily. The species of wood used can be specified. In this case, material kits and veneered sheets must be available in each of the species offered. In this case, the cell operator must either determine the species selected, or the species code that is part of the customer order must be matched with a bar coded material kit to ensure that the correct material is being processed.

The finish can also be selected from several available choices. This can be accomplished either by equipping the finish room with a separate system for each finish or by using a quick change system to switch from one finish to another. In a like manner, hinges and other visible hardware can be selected by the customer.

When you add together the various options we have discussed, you can see that the customer truly can customize the furniture to his or her liking. I envision design software systems where a three dimensional view of the furniture piece can be seen. This view will change to show any design changes as they are made.

The kitchen cabinet design package we work with currently shows a three-dimensional color view of the entire kitchen with the proper appliances, floor covering and wallpaper. Even the lighting type and location can be adjusted to see the effect of light and shadow on the kitchen design. Within this design, cabinets can be modified and adjusted until the exact combination is achieved.

I believe that shortly, this same type of program will be available for furniture design. The customer, either working at a retail outlet or off the Internet, will be able to view the piece of furniture in a realistic setting. They will be able to try various design changes, colors and styles until they are totally satisfied with the result. At that time, all the details of the selections made can automatically become part of the customer order. This electronic data can then be fed directly to the fabrication cell where the piece can be made exactly as ordered.

It is difficult to determine from this point, exactly where this will all lead. The furniture manufacturer can take some comfort in the fact that they will not have to create all the technology and perform all the software and integration work themselves.

In kitchen cabinets, my company already offers a complete integrated kitchen cabinet package, including the hardware, software, machine, fixtures, network and tooling. We also offer a similar package for cabinet face frames and five piece wood doors.

I expect that by the time you read this, we will also be offering a similar package for casegoods type furniture. The required technology will be pre-packaged with the required hardware, software and everything else needed to start furniture fabrication production.

Furniture fabrication will be a collaborative effort. The machine and technology supplier will need to work closely with the software and computer suppliers and with the customer. Companies using the system will also need to work together and share solutions to common problems so that they can all compete. To aid in this effort, Thermwood has established a technical forum within its web site thermwood.com.

Within this site, companies using the system can ask questions and exchange information and solutions to problems. The company will also participate by providing any information we have that might help answer questions or address problems.

This area of technology is moving very rapidly and will move even faster in the future. I believe that the somewhat scary ideas that I have expressed in this chapter will soon be an everyday part of our industry. To help move all of us into this new age, we will need to work together to develop, implement and share technical developments as quickly as possible.

# Chapter 8

## Design and Programming

# Chapter 8

## Design and Programming

Programming furniture fabrication cells seems to be the single biggest concern among furniture companies considering the concept. There is a common belief that a high-tech company can create and refine the required programs but that the average furniture company would be completely lost.

While this may have been true a few years ago, it is not true today. New tools and systems have been developed that make the programming task quite manageable, even for the average furniture company.

Before you begin programming entire furniture pieces using the newest technology, I feel it is important to understand the basics of programming. I don't think everyone reading this book needs to know the details of program creation, however, I do believe that they need to know the various systems that are used for programming.

I am not going to try and teach you how to program in this chapter. Instead, I will offer an overview of the various methods of creating CNC programs. I hope to generate an understanding of how each of these methods work and their relative advantages and shortcomings. When you complete this chapter, you should have a better fundamental understanding of this entire area than most people that create CNC programs for a living.

Programming has evolved over the years through several stages. Initially, programming consisted of creating the machine motions, one at a time, that were necessary to produce a part. Next, CAD/CAM systems were developed. Using CAD/CAM, the part required was designed and the system, rather than the programmer, created the machine motions necessary to cut the part. The latest advance are design systems where the final piece of furniture or a set of kitchen cabinets are designed and the system creates all the programs required for all the parts necessary to assemble the finished product.

The programming effort is very important. The overall operation and efficiency of the entire factory is determined by the fixtures and programs. They will determine just how efficient and profitable the operation will be.

In this chapter I will try and discuss all of the different methods of creating programs. I will start with basic methods of creating code for individual machine motions. I will offer an overview of CAD/CAM systems, including some detail on creating three-dimensional surfaces using five axis machines. I will then discuss the use of a common product design software package and show how it is used to create a complete set of components. Let us start with creating motions for an individual part.

There are a variety of methods of developing CNC programs for individual parts, each with advantages and disadvantages. To make things even more complex, many of these methods can be combined into an almost endless series of combinations.

I am not going to try and teach you how to program in this chapter. Learning to program a CNC router requires a book of its own. Instead, I am going to show you enough about programming for you to be able to understand the different methods used to create CNC programs in today's world.

I intend to explore this area in enough depth that you can understand subtle differences between specific code as executed by different controls when these differences have a material affect on the programming and use of the machine.

First, what is a CNC program? Today, a CNC program is a series of blocks of text. Each block of text is written in a specific format or structure that will be interpreted by the control. Each block of text will instruct the control to take some action.

Normally, each block of code is written on a separate line. On some controls line numbers will be shown, on others they will not.

The code is generally written in a format that is defined by an Electronic Industries Association standard. This standard is called EIA 274-D and it was initially intended to provide a consistent code format for NC controls built by different manufacturers.

When the standard was first developed, there was a great deal of concern over the possibility that the standard could stifle technical innovation. To keep this from happening, certain codes were reserved for future inclusion in the standard. In addition, certain codes were allowed freedom for each control manufacturer to define in any way they wished.

Control manufacturers have made extensive use of this freedom under the standard. In fact, they have made such extensive use of this freedom that few, if any, controls manufactured by different companies are code compatible. This means that code written for one machine will generally not run on another machine built by a different company. In fact, in some cases code written for one model machine will not run on another model machine even if controls for both machines were built by the same company.

NC code is sometimes called "M" and "G" code, because each block of text normally starts with the letter "M" or the letter "G". The letter "G" normally prefixes a machine motion line of code and the letter "M" generally prefixes an input, output or tooling control line of code.

There are two different methods of specifying axis motion, absolute and incremental. When the control is in the absolute mode, an axis position, X10.5 for example, specifies a position with respect to the home or 0,0 position of the axis. In this example, the position specified is 10.5 inches in the positive direction from the home position on the X Axis.

When the control is in the incremental mode, the code specifies a distance and direction to move the axis FROM THE CURRENT POSITION. Thus, the same code, X10.5 will produce a totally different motion depending on whether the control is in the absolute or incremental mode. In the absolute mode it will move to position 10.5 on the X Axis and in the incremental mode it will move 10.5 inches in the positive direction on the X Axis from its current position.

The absolute and incremental mode can be set using a "G" code. These codes are "modal" which means that whenever they are set, they remain active until changed.

There are many modal commands that remain in effect until reset. The speed of an axis, for example, is normally a modal command. Once the feed speed is set it will remain at that level unless reset. A good control will display the modal commands that are active at any time.

It is possible to switch between absolute and incremental modes within a program, but this can cause problems. It is very important to choose one mode that is normal, incremental for example. Then, anytime the absolute mode is used you must make certain that the code returns the control to the incremental mode before moving on or branching to another location.

A mistake in this area is a common reason for crashing a machine into a fixture. For example, let us assume we are at the 55 inch absolute position on the Y Axis and want to program a line of code to achieve a 2 inch motion to the left. The code for this is

G1Y2. "G1" indicates it is a linear motion and "Y2" indicates the motion is 2 inches in the positive direction on the Y Axis.

If the control is in the incremental mode it will, indeed, move 2 inches to the left. If, however, the machine was inadvertently left in the absolute mode, the axis would move 53 INCHES TO THE RIGHT! You can see how easy it is to crash the machine if you don't handle incremental and absolute modes properly.

G00 is the command for a rapid traverse linear motion. For example the line:

G00X10.5Y5.65

is a line of code that tells the control that we want a rapid motion with the X Axis moving 10.5 inches in the positive direction and the Y Axis moving 5.65 inches in the positive direction (we will assume the incremental mode from here on unless noted).

The results of this command will be different on different machines. Under EIA 274-D, the G00 command does not require linear interpolation. Linear interpolation is a feature where the control coordinates the motion of two or more axes so that they start and stop at the same time.

In this example, with linear interpolation, the machine will track a diagonal from the current position to a position 5.65 inches to the right and 10.5 inches forward of the last position. The path of the motion will be a straight line from the last position to the next.

Without linear interpolation, each axis is instructed to move as fast as possible from its own individual position to the next position without regard to what the other axes are doing. In this case, both the X and Y Axes would begin moving at the same speed until each had moved 5.65 inches. Then the Y Axis, which has already achieved its new position, would stop moving and the X Axis would continue until it moved a total of 10.5 inches.

The path traced would be a 45 degree diagonal for 5.65 inches along both the X and Y Axes and then an additional 4.85 inches along the X Axis. Why would you want to do this?

Actually, you don't. Linear interpolation requires sometimes-complex calculations to assure coordination between the axes that are moving. Early controls were too slow to perform these calculations at high feed speeds. The machines were required to move rather slowly so that the control could keep up the necessary calculations.

At times, however, it was desirable to move to another location quickly. Normally this was to re-position the head for another cut. The G00 command was used to free the control from the necessity of coordinating the axes so that higher feed speeds could be achieved.

With today's high-speed processors, coordinating the axes is no longer a limiting factor. On the other hand, not coordinating the axes can cause serious problems.

With coordinated or interpolated motion, you know the exact path that the machine will follow. Without interpolation, the path can be unpredictable. This unpredictable path is not normally a problem with a simple two-axis machine. The head is simply moved above the work and the path taken to the next position is not important. In this case there is nothing to crash into.

With a five-axis CNC router, many times the fixture is so high that you cannot get over the top of it. In this case, the path is very important. It would be quite easy for a non-interpolated positioning move to crash into the fixture. It makes no sense to have a G00 command that is not interpolated, even though interpolation is not strictly required by the standard.

Why have a G00 command at all?

Actually, the G00 command can be quite useful. This command is used to reposition the machine between cuts. Since we should not cut using this command, we can move as fast as the machine is capable of moving. In fact, the acceleration and deceleration rates can be increased beyond the point where smooth cutting motion occurs. This means faster motion between cuts and shorter overall cycle times.

Also, another feature of most controls is called "feed speed override". This normally consists of a knob that will either slow down or speed up the programmed feed speed on the machine while it is executing a program. The operator can use this knob to fine tune the feed speed to the actual material and cutting tools.

The G00 command is not affected by the position of the feed speed override control. Slowing the execution of the actual cuts will not slow the G00 repositioning motions.

The G00 command can be useful and will result in faster, more efficient programs. Make certain, however, that the control you are using provides full interpolation for this command even though it isn't an official requirement for the command.

I am not going to detail each of the "M" and "G" codes in this chapter but instead will focus on the various methods of creating programs that use these codes.

The most obvious and simple way of creating code is to sit down at a word processor and type each line of code required. Simple and easy, however, are not the same thing. Although this method creates code in a straightforward manner, it is all but impossible to envision the position and operation of a CNC router while working with a word processor.

This simple method can and is used to program straightforward two-axis motions. Even then, since the diameter of the tool must be taken into account, it is not particularly easy. Once the part requires three or more axes, it is all but impossible to create program code directly.

Perhaps the easiest way of creating program code is programming right at the machine, where the machine moves as the program steps are developed. In this way, you can see the resulting positions and paths and make any necessary corrections immediately.

This approach has other advantages. As part of the programming process it allows for the exact location of the fixture on the tabletop. It also allows for any positional inaccuracy of the machine itself. Some machines are not particularly accurate but are repeatable. These machines can produce consistent parts as long as they repeat accurately. When the machine is used to create the program, any machine inaccuracies are allowed for in the program. The only real disadvantage is that a program that allows for positioning inaccuracies of a machine will only function properly on that one machine. Programs of this type cannot be moved from one machine to another.

At this time I am going to introduce you to the Hand Held Programmer. This programming terminal was introduced by Thermwood in the late 1970s and remains a very powerful and popular programming tool.

The Hand Held Programmer looks like a large calculator. It has a keypad, a two-line display, a rotary positioning knob and an emergency stop button. It is plugged into the front of the control and is connected to the control by an umbilical cord. The Hand Held Programmer can be taken right to the machine where programs can be developed while you watch the results from close range.

The basic concept behind the Hand Held Programmer is quite simple. Just imagine a simple milling machine that uses hand cranks to move the table. Now imagine that you move the table to a position and then press a button to store that position. Then you move the table to a second position and again press the button to save that position. When the program runs, it moves from one saved position to the next.

This essentially is how the Hand Held Programmer works, except that instead of using the hand cranks to move the table we use the keys on the Programmer. To try and understand this a little better, let us imagine we are creating a program.

Let us assume we need to cut a more or less rectangular part. We have the part mounted to a fixture located somewhere in the center of the table.

We will use a 1/2 inch diameter router bit about an inch and a half long to trim the part. The first step is to move the head to the initial plunge point on the part. We will use the Hand Held Programmer to move the machine.

First select the axis you want to move. Type *Axis* then *1* to select the X Axis. To keep the number of keys to a minimum, numbers are used to designate the axes on the Hand Held Programmer. 1 is the X Axis, 2 the Y Axis, 3 the Z axis. On five axis machines, 4 and 5 are the two rotary head axes.

Now that we have selected the axis, type in the distance you want to move, 20 inches for example. Press the + key, indicating you want to move in the positive direction which is away from home on this axis. At that point the X Axis of the machine will move 20 inches. Now select *Axis 2* (Y Axis), type in a distance and press +. The Y Axis will move. Do the same for the Z Axis. We are now getting the head closer to the part.

At any time we can return to any axis we have already moved and change its position by adding to or subtracting from its position.

The display will indicate the active axis and the distance we have moved so far.

We are now only a few inches from the part. What we really want to do is to position the tool about an inch or so away from the part and then plunge into the part along the axis of the tool. When the program is started, the head will simply move away from home, position itself away from the part and then plunge straight into the part and begin trimming.

From an inch away from the part, it will be difficult to judge the exact plunge point so, instead we will move the tip of the tool right to the plunge point and then back it off an inch. This assures us that when we plunge, it will be in the proper location.

Since we are getting close to the part we will move in smaller increments. Type *Axis 1 .25* and press **+**. The X Axis will move .25 or ¼ of an inch. Press **+** again and it will move another ¼ of an inch. Each time you press the **+** or **−** key the axis will move ¼ of an inch since that was the last dimension you typed in.

Select *Axis 2* and type *.5*. Press **+**. The Y Axis will move ½ inch. Again, each time you press the **+** or **−** key the axis will move ½ inch. Now return to the X Axis and press **+**. It will move ¼ inch, not ½ inch. Each axis has its own default distance, which is the last distance you typed for that axis. Changing distance on another axis will not affect it.

Although this may sound a little complex, within just a few minutes it becomes quite natural and comfortable.

As you approach the part, there is another way to move the axis. There is a pulse wheel located at the bottom of the Hand Held Programmer. Turning this wheel clockwise will move the axis in the plus direction and turning the wheel counterclockwise will move the axis in the negative direction. As you rotate the pulse wheel you can feel individual detents at about one-degree increments. The distance that the axis moves for each of these detents can be adjusted by a series of keystrokes on the Hand Held Programmer.

We are now positioned with the tip of the router tool just touching the plunge point on the part. Now all we have to do is back off an inch.

There are a few things we should note at this point. First, the steps necessary to locate the head are more complex to describe than to actually do. An experienced Hand Held Programmer can actually locate the head properly in less time than it took you to read about it. At this point you should have an idea of how the Hand Held Programmer works.

There are many other features and techniques that have developed around the Hand Held Programmer. Key sequences are available for creating circles and arcs. Any three points can be turned into an arc, including free arcs in space.

At times it is necessary to execute a smooth flowing curve along a part. It would be quite difficult to program a large number of points very close together using the Hand Held Programmer and achieve a smooth, even motion. To address this requirement a capability from CAD/CAM systems has been added to the Hand Held Programmer toolbox. This capability is called a spline.

A spline is a mathematical function that takes a number of points and creates a smooth path through them. There are a number of different types of mathematical splines, but this can become much too involved for a discussion here. For our purposes, consider a spline a function that creates a smooth path through a series of points.

Splines initiated in boat building. The shape of the keel and hull of a boat were designed and small nails were driven into a wall to define the shape. A long, thin strip of wood about an eighth of an inch thick was then bent over the nails to define the smooth shape of the hull. This strip of wood was called a spline.

As the boat design process became more refined, mathematical functions were developed to replace the wood splines in defining a smooth curve through a series of points. These mathematical functions took on the name of the wood strip they replaced, the spline. As CAD/CAM systems developed, these mathematical functions became important tools for defining smooth curves and surfaces.

Thermwood has added spline capability to its control system in a couple of different forms. When you want a smooth curve through a series of points on a Thermwood control, you simply place a spline marker at the beginning of the points and a spline end marker at the end of the path. When executed, the control will calculate a spline, real-time, through the points.

Spline calculations are extremely involved. Even with today's very fast processors, they take time. For this reason, top speed when executing a spline that is being calculated real-time is limited. If you wish to cut at a higher speed, there is an alternative. A program with spline markers can be run through a utility called "CAD Path". This will generate a program where the spline is expanded in the same manner as a CAD/CAM system would expand a spline path. This expanded path can then be executed at any feed speed up to the limit of the machine. The "CAD Path" utility is part of Thermwood's 91000 SuperControl. I am not aware of any other control that has spline capability but there is no technical reason that it could not be added to these systems and I expect that they may be available for other systems in the future.

Spline capability and CAD Path bring CAD/CAM type programs to companies that create programs using the Hand Held Programmer. It does this without the need for a full CAD/CAM package, computer hardware and trained CAD/CAM programmers.

I have spent some time describing Hand Held Programming features. I have done this so that you know what to expect from this tool. Many companies programming flat parts and possibly the majority of companies programming three-dimensional trim parts today, program exclusively with the Hand Held Programmer. It is a very powerful tool and can be learned by almost anyone.

Because of their popularity, some CNC router manufacturing companies have introduced their own "Hand Held Programmer". Unfortunately, some of these are not much more than a utility box and a feed knob. If you plan to program at the machine, make certain that the programming terminal, Hand Held Programmer or whatever they call it has all the features you will need to do a quality, efficient job of creating programs. If this is to be your primary programming tool, make certain it is a good tool.

Now that you have had a glimpse of how the Hand Held Programmer works, you may have noticed something. It seems that the majority of programming time is spent trying to get the machine and head in the proper position. Most of the keystrokes are used to try and locate the desired point. Wouldn't it be nice if we could simply guide the machine into position by hand and then enter the point? Now you can.

In 1997, Thermwood introduced a programming probe, which does essentially that. On three axis machines the Probe mounts to the side of the main router head. On five axis machines the probe mounts to the router spindle where the router bit would normally be located. The probe is about six inches long and four inches in diameter and will make the router head about six inches longer than normal. The offset, will be removed using either tool length compensation or fixture offset so that the actual router bit will travel the path defined by the probe when the resulting program is run.

The probe is used by inserting a probe tip into the probe body. The probe tip is the same size and shape as the router bit we intend to use. This probe tip is then used to guide the machine around a part.

The probe tip moves slightly from side to side and in and out of the probe body. These movements are translated by the probe into electronic signals that are fed to the machine control. These signals are used to move the three linear axes of the machine.

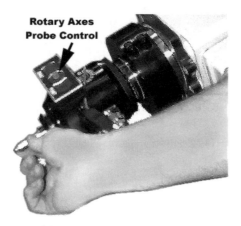

There are three modes in which the probe can be used. The first of these is the "point mode". In the point mode, the probe is used to move the machine axes to a point much like the Hand Held Programmer was used to move the machine to a desired point. When the point is reached, a record button on the probe is pressed and the control creates the line of NC code necessary to move from the last recorded point to the current position. Move to the next position and press the record button again. This process is continued until all the points necessary have been recorded.

As you can see, this process is much faster than recording the exact same points using only the Hand Held Programmer. By the way, the Hand Held Programmer can be plugged in and used at the same time that the probe is being used. For example, the probe could be used to locate a plunge point. Then the Hand Held Programmer could be used to back the head away from the part, record the point and then return to the plunge point. The probe could then be used to continue programming. In another example, the probe could be used to locate the edge of a circle. The actual circle can then be programmed using the Hand Held Programmer. A circle programmed with the Hand Held Programmer will be much more accurate than one developed with the probe alone.

As you can see, in the point mode, the probe is an extremely useful tool that makes program development much faster and easier.

How does the machine know the position of the probe tip? This is not as simple a question as you might think. First, the control can look at the position of all axes and determine the exact location of the machine head. This, however, is not the position of the probe tip. As you recall, the probe tip moves slightly to provide the input signal to generate machine motion. If we simply use the position of the head as defined by the axes positions, we are assuming that the probe tip is exactly centered. In actual practice, it may not be perfectly centered when we record a point.

Since we are using the probe tip to define a position, we must determine the exact position of the probe tip and not the position of the machine axes.

The probe system that Thermwood uses has three very accurate linear scales that measure exactly how far off center the probe tip is in three perpendicular axes inside the probe body. This offset information is sent to the machine control. The control then takes the position of all machine axes, the offsets from the probe and calculates the exact position of the probe tip. On five-axis machines, the control must also take into account the rotational position of the two rotary head axes. As you can imagine this is a rather involved calculation.

I have included some information on exactly how the probe works because most people that use the probe find it so simple that they totally underestimate the underlying technology.

The second basic mode in which the probe operates is called the "drag mode". The drag mode is used to define a curved path in space using only the probe. There are actually a number of different ways of programming a free curved path in space. The method that is best depends somewhat on the application and requirements.

The most straightforward method of creating this path is by using the drag mode and the programming probe. To use this method the probe is moved to the beginning point of the path we wish to program. This is normally done using the point mode. At this point we activate the drag mode by pressing the drag button on the probe.

The goal in programming a smooth curved path in space is to create a program that consists of a series of very short line segments that connect to one another and define the path. If these segments are short enough without abrupt changes in direction, the resulting program will appear to be a smooth, continuous curved line in space.

To achieve this smooth path, typically the line segments are quite short, ten to twenty thousandths of an inch for example. Because the segments are short and there may be thousands of them, it is not possible to enter these segments one at a time.

In the drag mode the probe creates this type of program. The way the probe works is a bit less direct, however. When you activate the drag mode, the probe begins recording the position of all axes very quickly. Although this record interval can be adjusted, it is normally set at about six milliseconds. Every six milliseconds the control records the position of all axes whether the axes have moved or not. During this time, the operator is tracing the path using the probe. This tracing process is generally done slowly and carefully.

When the drag mode is turned off, the actual program code is developed by the control. The control now has a stored list of the position of each axis throughout the tracing process. To convert this list into a NC program, the control creates a block of code for the start point of the path. It then begins calculating the distance that the tool tip moved for each set of axes positions that has been recorded. When the combined movement is equal to the segment length, the control again writes a line of code to move from the last point to the current point. The value of this segment length can be specified. It then discards all the points used to reach this position and begins the process again, defining another segment. It continues the process, using the recorded axes positions to define set length segments until the entire path has been programmed.

The result of this process is a program that consists of a series of generally equal size segments connected together along the desired path. The program is essentially the same as a program generated by a good quality CAD/CAM system.

In practice, three axis programs work extremely well. Defining a complex path using the probe and only linear axes is easy. On five-axis machines, if a rotary axis motion is added to the linear axes during the segment, it becomes a bit more difficult to get the smooth, professional program you are looking for. The probe and control are more than capable of handling input from all five axes simultaneously. The difficulty that occurs is with smoothly coordinating the linear and rotary axes by hand. Some people are able to do this rather easily while others never do seem to get an acceptable path. Luckily, there is a simple way of achieving a virtually perfect path that combines both linear and rotary axes.

We will now go back and record a series of points along the path using the point mode. In this way, all the axes can be positioned slowly and carefully using the probe, and if necessary the Hand Held Programmer. Depending on how quickly the orientation changes, these points can be anywhere from a quarter of an inch to an inch or more apart. After the points have been entered, a spline marker is entered in front of and at the end of the line segment.

After the program has been completed, it will be processed through a utility in the control called CADpath. CADpath will create another program where the points between the spline markers are converted into a CAD/CAM type path with short, connecting line segments. The final result is essentially the exact same output you would get from a full blown CAD/CAM system, yet the process can be completed by a machine programmer that is not trained in the operation of a complex CAD/CAM computer system.

The reason that CADpath does not modify the current program is in case you need to modify or edit the path. Should you find that a point or two needs to be adjusted, it is quite easy to take the original program with a limited number of original points and adjust it. Then, simply run it through CADpath again and you have an edited version, quickly and easily. If we had modified the original program, there may be thousands of points and editing would be much more difficult.

With CADpath it is easy for almost anyone to create smooth professional programs that exactly match the part. The high tech world of CAD/CAM programming has been made simple enough that almost anyone can do it.

The third mode that the probe can execute is the scan mode. The scan mode is used to create a program to reproduce a surface by making a cut, stepping over a slight amount and returning. The machine runs back and forth over the part, stepping over a little bit each time until the entire surface has been cut.

The probe and the scan mode can be used with a physical model to create the necessary program. To operate in the scan mode, the perimeter of the part is defined and the step-over distance is specified. The scan process is then started.

The machine and the probe will automatically move back and forth over the model, accurately tracing it while creating a meta-file. The meta-file is much like the list of axes positions that we discussed earlier. It contains the axes positions recorded every few milliseconds. The logic and motions needed to trace the part will vary depending on how radical the surface variations are. If steep walls must be climbed or deep valleys followed, the movement speed of the tracing process is automatically slowed. Because of the rather involved calculations necessary to convert these paths into program code, it is much faster to simply copy the axes positions and process it than to try and both control the machine motion and process the program at the same time.

The scan mode is commonly used to create custom moldings, initial carving surfaces and curved surfaces such as a sculpted drawer front or a Bombay chest.

The programming processes we have just covered are generally done at the machine. This has some major advantages since the actual part and actual machine are used to create the program, generally accuracy is quite good, even for machines that are not particularly accurate or well aligned. To function properly, the machine must be repeatable, but if the part is programmed at the machine, the machine does not have to be accurate. There is a major difference between accuracy and repeatability.

The next evolutionary step in programming technology was the development of the CAD/CAM system. When first introduced they were expensive, complex and limited in their capability. They were used by the defense and aerospace industries, but few other companies turned to these systems for program development because they were complex, cost millions of dollars and really didn't work very well. That has all changed today.

Today, CAD/CAM systems are available at a variety of prices, can operate on reasonably inexpensive computers and are quite capable. In the next few pages, I am going to try and offer an overview of systems available today, including costs and technical requirements. Since this is a rapidly moving field, some of this information will become obsolete rather quickly. You might want to note the publication date of this book to determine just how far behind it might be at the time you are reading it.

The basics of CAD/CAM will, however, generally remain constant so much of what I will talk about should still be accurate regardless of the publication date.

Before we discuss specific CAD/CAM systems, I would like to explain the fundamentals of how a traditional CAD/CAM system works. From an understanding of the basic operation, we can then discuss the various modifications that certain system vendors have made to the basic operation.

CAD stands for **C**omputer **A**ided **D**esign. CAM stands for **C**omputer **A**ided **M**anufacturing. Although the two sets of letters are commonly used together, they represent two different functions. Let us start with CAD.

The CAD portion of the package is used to design the part. To help us understand this, we will explain how a very simple two-dimensional part would be designed and programmed using a CAD/CAM system.

For our example we will make a square with rounded corners like this:

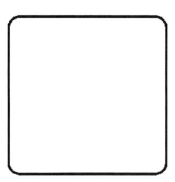

The first step is to design the part using the CAD system. CAD systems all have a simple system for creating a square and specifying its size. We now have a design that looks like this:

Now we must round the corners. CAD systems have a command, normally called the "fillet", with which you can specify a radius and then simply point to the junction of two lines. The square corner between the lines will be replaced with a curve, with the specified radius that smoothly blends the lines together.

Applying the fillet command to each corner gives us our part, a square with rounded corners.

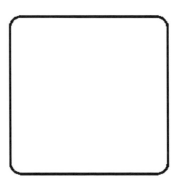

We have now designed the part. Depending on the CAD system, this information can be saved in a number of different formats. Some of these formats are used by multiple systems and others are used by only one package. If your CAD system can use one of the standard formats, the AutoCAD DXF format for example, then the design you create can be moved from one system to another. This is a useful feature even if you only plan to use one system. Should you decide to use outside programming help or want to upgrade your system in the future, you will be happy you selected a system that is generally compatible.

At this point, the work of the CAD system is done. If we want to develop an NC program to manufacture the part on a machine, we need a CAM system. Let me explain the things we need to do to the existing part design to create a machine program.

If you recall, we designed the part by creating a square and then filleting the corners, one at a time. The design data will be made up of four lines and four arcs. Since we created the square first, the four lines will appear first on a list of design features. The order of the lines on that list will depend on which direction we created the square. The four lines will be followed by four arcs. The order of the arcs on the list is determined by the order in which you specified the fillet commands.

If you simply use this list of design features to machine the part, the machine would first machine the four lines, one at a time and then it would cut the four rounded corners. The direction of cut would not necessarily be correct. This is not what we want.

To properly cut the part, we want to start at a point off the part and move into the part cutting in the proper direction. We then want to move smoothly around the part, first cutting a line, then the arc, then the next line until we traveled completely around the part one time.

To accomplish this, we will need to rearrange the order of the design features that we programmed. We may also need to swap the direction of some of the lines or arcs so that they are drawn in the direction we want to cut.

This is the first major job of the CAM system. It orders the geometry and cut direction and links the geometric entities together. We now have a smooth continuous line around the part in the correct direction, made up of the lines and arcs we developed in the design process. Can we now use this to program the machine?

Not quite yet. The lines represent the edge of the part. A machine program, however, defines the path taken by the center of the cutting tool. If we try and use the lines we developed as the cut path, the diameter of the cutting tool will make the part too small.

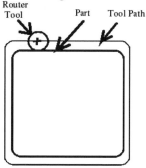

We must shift the cut path away from the part an amount equal to the radius of the cutter. In this way, the edge of the cutter will trace along the edge of the part. This is another major task for the CAM system.

Each CAM system works a little differently, however, they must all reorder the data, set the cut direction and offset the cutter. Once all this has been done, the result is generally known as centerline data. It is a set of data defining the path that the center of the tool is to take. It is still not a machine program.

The final part of this package is known as the post processor. The post processor is a program written for a specific machine that translates the centerline data into NC code for that machine. We now have a program that will run on the machine.

Post processors can be quite simple, for a two-axis machin, or can be extremely involved for a full five-axis machine. On a five axis machine, the post processor must not only know the syntax of the NC code required by the control, but must also know the mechanical configuration of the machine itself. The centerline data defines the path that the tool must take. The post processor must then calculate the movement of all five axes required to achieve the defined path with the tip of the tool. This makes a five-axis post processor a rather involved program.

Here, in a very simplified form, is the operation of a CAD/CAM system. The CAD design package designs the part and outputs geometric data. The CAM package creates a file that defines the path for the centerline of the tool in order to cut the part and a post processor converts the centerline data to an NC program that can run on the machine.

Now that we have some idea of how a CAD/CAM system works, let us look at the various types of CAD/CAM systems available.

In general, CAD/CAM systems can be separated into two major categories, those that work with two-dimensional parts and designs and those that work with three-dimensional designs.

Obviously all parts are three-dimensional. From a CAD standpoint, however, a two-dimensional part has its design features defined by the X and Y Axes. The Z Axis or part thickness is generally a fixed distance with Z Axis motion being simple plunge and retract motions.

We will begin our discussion by looking at systems for designing simple flat parts with a three-axis CAD/CAM system. These systems are called three axis CAD/CAM because they are intended to program three axis machines. In general they will develop path data for two of the three axes and will provide plunge and retract data for the third axis.

There are a number of relatively low cost three-axis systems available in the market today. They work essentially the way we described earlier using our square with rounded corners.

There are also a number of CAD-only programs, such as AutoCAD, that can design parts. These are not full CAD/CAM systems since they do not have the programs needed to perform the CAM functions. There is, however, a method of using these systems as a full CAD/CAM package by using a unique feature of Thermwood's 91000 SuperControl.

This feature, called a DXF translator, will work with any CAD system that can output its geometry in an AutoCAD compatible DXF file format. DXF is a file format for CAD generated geometry that was first developed by AutoCAD. This format became widely accepted and many CAD systems have the ability to output files in the DXF format.

To make the Thermwood DXF Translator work, the CAM data is added to the CAD drawing using text statements. To make the system work, we must specify the location of the plunge, the direction of cut and which side of the line the cutter is on. To accomplish this, a text statement in a fixed format is written across a line in the drawing. The endpoint nearest the text statement will be the plunge point. The direction of cut is the direction from the endpoint toward the text statement. The location of the text statement on the drawing has already provided two of the needed pieces of information.

The text statement itself contains a sequence number in case more than one path is to be cut. It also contains a "G" code indicating which side of the line the cutter is to be offset. At this point, all the necessary information is available.

When the file is run through the DXF Translator in the Thermwood control, the control will automatically reorder the geometric data and create the appropriate program to machine the part. It is also possible to add any other commands to the text statement. The control will execute these commands before executing the actual path motion.

This system allows relatively low cost CAD systems to operate as full CAD/CAM systems when a two-dimensional tool path is all that is necessary. When we need to program and run a full five-axis machine, things get a little more complex.

There are two basic machining functions for a five-axis CNC router. The first is to trim a molded part, such as a plastic part or a formed plywood piece, along a trim line. This can include cutting out openings in a part as well as removing flash from the perimeter.

The second basic function of a five-axis CNC router is to machine surfaces such as those found on patterns or molds.

Things can get a little confusing here since three-dimensional parts, such as moldings and carvings, can be machined on three axis machines. Only when undercuts are required or when the tool must approach the work from a direction other than above is a five axis machine required. One example of this is trimming molded plywood seats. Trimming these parts normally requires that the tool remain perpendicular to the seat all around the cut line. This requires a five-axis machine.

While the same CAD/CAM systems are used for both trimming and pattern making, the methods that are used and the features required of the system are somewhat different for each application. We will first address the part trimming application and then talk about programming and machining surfaces.

When we consider trimming a part, we will need to match a trim program to a real world part. This can be more of a problem than it appears on the surface.

To program a trim line using a CAD/CAM system requires that either the part geometry or at least the trim line geometry and head vectors be available. It is a common error to assume that if the original part was designed using a CAD system, the necessary geometry already exists.

In molded plywood for example, almost never does the actual part size exactly match the size developed using the CAD system. Variations in pattern making, mold making, part shrinkage and machine absolute accuracy result in parts that are close, but not exactly what was intended. In most cases, these variations are significant enough that if the original CAD design is used to generate the trim line, the resultant trimmed part is not commercially acceptable.

This means that, in most cases, you will need to somehow modify or replace existing part geometry data with data describing the actual part size before an acceptable trim path can be developed using a CAD/CAM system. There are two methods I am aware of for doing this. The first is by using some type of coordinate measuring machine to measure the actual part. These machines, although quite expensive, can very accurately measure a trimmed part and provide most CAD systems with the necessary points needed to generate accurate geometry. This will correct for all accumulated errors that occurred up to the point where the part was complete and ready to trim. It will not account for absolute positioning errors in the actual trimming machine itself.

Another less costly but somewhat less accurate method of obtaining real world points is to use a three-dimensional computer input device. These input devices are normally jointed arm designs that input to the computer the three Cartesian coordinates of the tip of the arm.

A trimmed part is placed near the arm and the tip of the input device is used to pick up points along the trim path. It can also be used to pick up points on a surface so that the CAD system can recreate the surface.

Many times all points on a part cannot be reached by the arm without moving the part. In this case, reference points can be established on the part, then the part moved and the reference points again located. Software within the system will then blend the points together. In this way, a part can be moved around as needed to be able to input all necessary points.

These input arms are available from several sources and can be obtained with arms that range from about a foot long to about three feet long. They vary in cost from a few thousand dollars to about twenty thousand dollars.

In general, input arms can locate a position within its working envelope to somewhere between ten and twenty thousandths of an inch.

Another method of obtaining actual geometric points is to use the CNC router itself in conjunction with a Hand Held Programmer or Programming Probe to pick up the points from an actual molded part. These points not only take into account variation in the part from design to final part but also variation in the trimming machine. There are, however, several cautions about this approach.

First, a machine generated point is not geometric data. Instead it is an "M" and "G" code program describing the position of each axis of the machine. A type of reverse post processor is needed to translate these axis positions back to a geometric point in space. These programs, designed to back feed machine points are not common, so make certain that software is available for any machine you intend to use in this manner.

Another area to consider is overall machine positioning accuracy. We stated earlier that this method of picking up points using the machine does correct for any machine inaccuracy and this, in fact, is true. This correction, however, is only good if the next time the part is run, it is machined on the exact same machine and is located in the exact same location on that machine as when the points were first generated. If the machine has any significant inaccuracy, the resulting trim program will only operate properly on that one machine. If the program is moved to another machine with different positioning accuracy, the resulting trim path may be far enough off that the part is unusable.

Building an accurate five-axis machine is quite involved. There are many machines in the market where the positioning accuracy is such that programs developed using one machine will not execute properly on any other machine, even the same model from the same manufacturer. Needless to say, generally these machines will not be able to properly execute programs developed using off-line CAD/CAM systems and coordinate measuring machines. To utilize this type of machine, it is mandatory that the program be developed using the machine itself and that the program be restricted to operating on only that one machine.

If your tolerances are wide enough and the CNC router accuracy is tight enough, it may be possible to develop trim programs that will be able to execute, unchanged, on two or more machines. In many thermoforming applications, Thermwood five-axis CNC routers routinely share the same program so I know it is possible in real world production. Many customers I have talked to, however, significantly underestimate the difficulty in doing something as simple as moving a program from one machine to another. This area can be quite complex.

Once you have actual part geometry, there are several options depending on the CAD/CAM system you are using. Some CAD/CAM systems restrict program motions to the three major axes of the machine. They allow the head to be positioned and then perform the actual cut using only the linear axes. These systems are five-axis CAD/CAM systems but are three-axis versions of five-axis systems. The three axis limitation is not necessarily a problem if the machine being programmed is also restricted to three axis simultaneous motions. The limitation to both the machine and the CAD/CAM system, however, results in less efficient programs at best, and may mean that certain parts cannot be trimmed at all in the worst case.

Several CAD/CAM vendors have added a capability to their products to create a true five-axis simultaneous motion using a cut line and head vectors. These systems start with full part geometry. To this is added the trim line. Along the trim line, vectors defining the head orientation are specified. The system then creates a trim program where the tool tip follows the trim line and the head orientation moves smoothly through the defined vectors.

Another similar method of developing a trim path is to create a surface. This is in essence a three-dimensional model of the part. A trim path is then projected onto the surface. The orientation of the head to the part surface is then specified. The program then creates a tool path where the tool tip runs through the projected trim line and the head maintains the specified orientation to the surface of the part.

For example, you could define the tool path and specify that the head remains perpendicular to the part surface being trimmed. The system would then create a trim path where the tool tip traveled along the trim path and the head remained perpendicular to the surface of the part throughout the cut.

Another approach used by some CAD/CAM systems is called the ruled surface trim. This approach does not require complete part geometry. Instead, the trim line must be defined in space. From this line, a second offset line is defined away from the part and away from the trim line. It is assumed that a vector from one line to the other is the vector along which the head lays. The system then creates a program where the tool tip travels along the defined trim line and the head is oriented along the offset line.

Another approach is to define the trim line in space and then, at various points along the line, a vector defining the head orientation is specified. The system then creates a trim path where the tool tip travels along the trim path and the head moves smoothly from one defined orientation to the next. Some companies call this synchronized programming.

Earlier we talked about Thermwood's CADpath program. This system is quite similar to the synchronized programming we just described. With it, points are picked up along the trim path using the probe or hand held. These points define both the trim path and the head vectors. Then, without having to convert these points to geometry and back, the CADpath program generates a ready-to-run trim program. The full five axis trim program moves the tool tip through the trim path while smoothly changing the head orientation through the defined points. The CADpath program is a standard part of the Thermwood control and requires no additional investment. Also, the CADpath program requires much less training and technical expertise than is required to operate a full CAD/CAM package.

These are the most popular method currently used to create trim programs using CAD/CAM systems. All methods are not available from all vendors. Also, some vendors sell a very basic system and then add some of the capabilities and features we have just described at an extra cost. As this book is being written, systems that operate using the methods just described cost somewhere between $6,000 and $50,000.

The second major application for CAD.CAM systems is in generating surfaces. These surfaces can be combined together to generate programs to machine patterns or moldings. As you might imagine, creating a program to machine a surface is quite a bit more complex than generating trim lines.

There are two reasons for generating a surface program. One is to manufacture a product in volume where a surface must be machined into the product. The second is to create a single example of a design such as a pattern or mold.

If you need to produce a volume of parts with surface machining and if a sample of the surface already exists, Thermwood's probe has a scan mode where it can scan the sample and create a program that can reproduce the surface on a production basis. This same process is extensively used in the furniture industry to program carved wood parts for high-end solid wood furniture.

If, however, you are trying to machine the first article of a new design, a sample does not exist so it is not normally possible to use the probe and scan the surface. In this case you must design the part and develop the program using a CAD/CAM system.

CAD/CAM systems intended to work with three-dimensional parts come in two, three, four and five axis versions, even though all may be able to program a full five-axis machine. Generally, the two-axis systems are the lowest cost. As additional axes are added, each step further increases the system cost. To understand this, we will need to talk about the different ways of developing a machined surface.

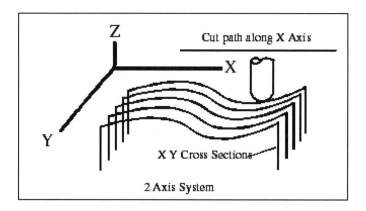

Let us start with a two-axis system. A typical two-axis system uses cross sections of the part to be machined to determine the path of the head. In a two-axis system, these cross sections must lay along one of the axes of the machine. For example, the cross-section could include the X and Z Axes. To cut this cross-section, the head is oriented and the Y Axis is set. Then, the X and Z Axes move to trace the particular cross section shape. When the cross section is complete, the Y Axis shifts over a set amount and the cross section for that new Y position is again traced using the X and Z Axes.

X and Z cross sections for each point along the Y Axis are cut until the entire surface has been machined. You will note that during this entire process, only the X and Z Axes were used to develop the surface cuts.

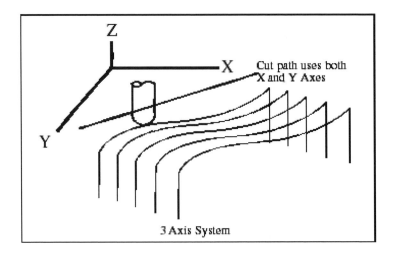

A three-axis system works in the same way, except the cross section does not need to lie along an axis of the machine. The cuts can be diagonals using both the X and Y Axes. Again, the head steps over each pass but this time the step over is perpendicular to the cross cut direction.

The examples we have covered are known as single surface parts. That is, the design is made up of only one surface. If multiple surfaces need to be machined using a single surface CAD/CAM package, each surface needs to be programmed and executed separately. The area between the surfaces that blends from one surface to the other must then be finished in some manner.

If you want to be able to design a part with multiple surfaces and machine the blend or transition areas between the surfaces, you need to upgrade to a multiple surface CAD/CAM package.

This package will create smooth transitions between different surfaces after you define the surface. With most CAD/CAM packages multiple surface capability is an extra cost option or add-on to the basic package.

In each of the packages described so far, we have been working with two or three axes. The actual cuts are performed with the head in a fixed position. The head position can be reoriented between cuts but the head cannot be moved during the actual machining operation. To add the ability to move the head during the machining operation we need to move to a four or five axis CAD/CAM system.

With these more advanced systems come more capabilities. It is now possible to perform, what is commonly known as flow line surfaces. When executing flow line surfaces, the system tries to keep the head perpendicular to the surface being machined within a specified range. This can be useful when using shaped or flat bottom cutters to provide smoother surface finishes. For an additional cost, lead-lag can be added to the package. Lead-lag capability means that the head is not exactly perpendicular to the surface, but instead leads or lags the surface by a fixed angle.

This can be useful when performing machining functions where the tool must be angled slightly to provide some type of machining clearance. Cutting aluminum honeycomb is a good example of this.

Honeycomb is machined using a cutter that looks very much like a gasoline engine valve. For this reason it is called a valve stem cutter. This cutter must be tilted a few degrees into the part so that the trailing edge is slightly above the surface that was cut with the leading edge. Not only does this keep the trailing edge from bending or turning down the edges of the honeycomb but it helps to lift the cut material from the part. Lead-lag capability is quite important in this type of application.

Again, with full five-axis systems you can have single surface or multiple surface capability. Another upgrade for multiple surface capability is multiple surface flow line capability. This means that not only does the system generate the transitions between surfaces, but also allows flow line machining of the transition areas. A further enhancement is gouge checking.

With gouge checking, the system checks the tool and head to make certain that in machining one surface and trying to stay perpendicular, it does not hit or gouge out another surface or area on the part. Without gouge checking, a problem of this type results in either a gouged out part or a head crash.

When a lower cost system with gouge checking detects interference, it alerts the operator or programmer. It is then the responsibility of the operator or programmer to modify the program to eliminate the problem. High-end systems can modify the programs automatically by changing the angle of attack to eliminate the interference problem.

Another feature of some CAD/CAM systems is called trimmed surfaces. When using the trimmed surfaces feature on a part with two or more surfaces, it allows the programmer to create oversized, overlapping surfaces and then trim them to fit together. This can be quite a bit easier than attempting to develop exactly sized surfaces and then fitting them together.

Another method of creating a surface is called NURBS. NURBS stands for Non Uniform Rationalized B-Spline. This is a very complex name for a very simple idea.

Using NERBS, a surface is defined by defining the paths that surround the surface. For example, four curved lines could be connected at the corners. This system then creates a surface that flows to connect the four lines smoothly. Although there is a lot of very high-end math involved in the creation of the surface, NURBS offers the programmer an easy way to develop a smooth flowing transition between known lines.

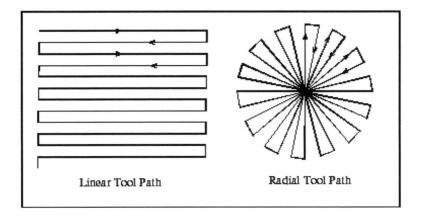

Linear Tool Path          Radial Tool Path

Each of the systems we have discussed so far have used linear tool paths. Some companies call this parallel machining. It simply means that the cut paths are straight lines parallel to each other, each offset from the last. There is another method of machining called radial tool path that may work better on certain parts. In radial tool path, the cutting path is a straight line from a center point to an outer radius and then back to the center. Each time the path starts from the center point but goes out on a slightly different angle like the spokes of a wheel. It continues shifting the angle until it goes out at every radial of a complete circle.

The choice between linear tool paths or radial tool paths depends on the shape and surfaces of the part. In some cases one method or the other will give you significantly smoother surfaces to work with by reducing steps on nearly vertical surfaces. This results in significantly less post finishing of the part.

In either case, however, unless the steps are made extremely small, some sanding or post finishing will be needed. If you use very small steps, the cycle times can become extremely long and in most cases, cost more in machine time than the required post finishing. The balance between more machining time and finishing time will vary with each company and each application.

So far in our discussion of CAD/CAM programming, we have been talking about programming the finished surface of the part. There is another area of programming that is almost as important. This area is roughing.

Roughing or broaching is the process of removing the bulk of material from a part blank so that the finish program is only required to remove a small amount of material to achieve the final, smooth surface.

These roughing programs tend to remove material in much coarser steps than the finish program. Almost every CAD/CAM system uses a separate set of menus and programs to create the roughing program. On higher performance systems, it is only necessary to define the maximum cut and the offset of the roughing program from the finish surface. The system then develops the roughing program to cut away the bulk of material from the blank. The result of roughing is a part that is slightly larger than the finished piece. The amount that the rough part is oversize varies depending on a number of factors. Typically the rough part is at least .030 to .060 inch oversize and can be a half an inch or more oversized in some materials. To achieve a smooth final product, however, the roughed blank should not be so large that significant cutting forces are developed during the finish cuts. These high cutting forces can result in degraded surface quality and "push-off" where the tool and head flex in reaction to the cutting force. The balance between rough cut and finish cut comes with experience.

One of the newest approaches to program generation is automatic programming. While this is not an official name for the practice, it does accurately describe the process.

Automatic programming is generally limited to a type of part or a family of parts. The best example of this is the machining of kitchen cabinet boxes.

Software packages currently exist that allow an entire kitchen to be designed on a PC, sometimes in full three dimension. As the cabinet sizes and locations are specified, you can see exactly what they will look like. When you complete the design, the task of creating machine programs for all the parts of all the cabinets still remains.

Kitchen cabinets have one important characteristic that lends itself to automatic programming. That characteristic is that they are common. By common, I mean that they are all machined and assembled in essentially the same way. Sure, the size and shelf location may vary, but most of the design features are essentially standard and common between cabinet boxes.

Because of this commonality, once the variables such as size, number and location of shelves, etc are defined, it becomes possible to automatically create the programs needed to machine all the parts. The computer can even nest the parts on 4 by 8 sheets of material to offer the best yield.

These systems are available for several applications today. With them, a final product is specified and the system automatically creates the necessary programs to make the parts needed to build that product.

The systems used for kitchen cabinet design can currently be used to create the programs necessary to build case good type furniture. The system offered by Thermwood even has a system to produce the hardwood frames for the face of the product as well as five-piece hardwood doors. This system, cabinet software with hardwood frames and doors is currently being used to design and program furniture case goods simply because it is so fast and easy. I have been encouraging the companies that supply cabinet design software to add the features needed for furniture fabrication programming of case goods. Perhaps by the time you are reading this book, these systems will already be available.

These types of product design packages are possible because the basic structure, construction and layout of the product is fixed. Take a kitchen cabinet, for example. It consists of a top, bottom, two sides and a back. The top and bottom attach to the sides and back in a fixed manner. Although the manner of attaching the pieces can vary from company to company, it seldom varies within a company. The cabinet may have drawers or doors and one or more shelves.

If you carefully look at the details of the overall design, you find that the features can be divided into two categories. The first category includes those features that will change on virtually every piece made. These include the height, width, number of doors, shelves, etc.

The second category are those features that seldom change. These include the fastening method between components, the method by which shelves are mounted, the door or drawer hardware design and mounting position and the like.

The product design software starts by allowing you to define those features that seldom change. This effort is generally completed only once although the various choices can always be changed. It then allows you to design new pieces by only defining those few items that vary every time a piece is built.

When you specify those items that change, the height, width, number of shelves, drawers, etc., the system applies the remainder of the design details from the pre-programmed data and is then able to create programs to machine all the required parts. The overall effort required seems small because each time only a few new dimensions need be specified. The task of applying the hundreds of detailed design features each time is handled automatically.

This is a simple concept, although it is very powerful. The software that accomplishes this is actually quite sophisticated.

There are numerous aids available to even further simplify the task of selecting the few features that may vary. For example, you may specify a standard height for a base cabinet. When a base cabinet is specified, it shows up already at that standard height. It may then only be necessary to specify a width to obtain a final design. Of course, if you want to change the height you can, but it starts out at, what the system believes will be the most likely choice for the height.

Most cabinet design software packages then output the various parts, nested on a sheet. They generally output the pieces in the DXF format we discussed earlier. While it is possible to simply execute the output file as presented, there are some difficulties in doing this.

Many of the problems we discussed in simply pulling design data from a CAD package also apply here. In addition, the data commonly appears on a per part basis. This means that all the motions needed to make the first part and grouped together, then the motions for the second part, and the third and so forth. If you execute these, the machine will completely machine the first part, including all the necessary tool changes before it goes to the second part, where it also changes the same tools again. By the end of the sheet, a considerable amount of time has been spent changing tools.

A better approach is to select the first tool and then perform all the machining using that tool on all the parts. Then change to the second tool and perform all the second tool machining on all the parts. The result is a substantially faster cycle time.

Just as with the CAD/CAM system, the way to accomplish this is to move the CAD data into a CAM system. The parts can then be grouped and the machine motions and tool selections optimized.

Although most machine companies use this approach, Thermwood has taken this one step farther. The functions that the

CAM system performs are the same on every sheet. The nested parts may be different, but the functions performed by the CAD system are always the same, therefore, the CAM functions can be made totally automatic.

There is no reason to move the data into a general purpose CAM package. Since the functions are always the same, the CAM functions can be made totally automatic.

In accomplishing this, Thermwood decided to go directly into the part database rather than using the DXF output because this allowed for additional features and capability. The final result, however, can be somewhat confusing. The CAM functions, which are necessary, happen almost instantly in the background. This can confuse people who expect to see or initiate a CAM function that magically doesn't seem to be needed. The CAM function is needed, it just happens automatically.

At this point, I am going to present one possible approach to creating programs for furniture fabrication. This approach is one that my company is just beginning to develop as this is being written. It addresses a series of concerns, both technical and political.

Companies interested in furniture fabrication want a programming system that can develop the necessary part programs as easily and quickly as possible. At the same time, they want a high level of design freedom to create the designs that their furniture designers develop.

To create a system that easily produces programs for products such as kitchen cabinets, the basic structure and structural design of the product is somewhat in the control of the software company. Within the basic software package, the end customer can modify the assembly techniques. Once the basic construction techniques have been developed, the customer can then easily customize the product size.

This type of system works well when the product is a simple, frameless cabinet. When we try and use it to produce case goods, a new set of problems develop.

Most furniture is made of both panels and solid wood components. A method must be found to create the necessary programs for these wood components.

In addition, different types of furniture have different styles or design features. These design elements vary tremendously, making it nearly impossible for the programming software company to accommodate them all.

If the software supplier attempts to provide design elements, several problems develop. First, the available offering will always be limited to what they offer. Also, it would be quite easy for your competitor to simply choose the same design off the same software package and produce the exact same product. For most furniture companies this is not acceptable.

To address these problems, provide a high level of design and styling freedom and still make programming relatively easy, we have developed a new approach toward case goods furniture program development.

The key concept to this new approach is to separate a part into its structural properties and its style properties.

Structural properties include the part's size, thickness, and assembly features such as mortise or tenon joints. Style properties are the design or style features of a part such as a shaped edge, vein line or carving.

In this approach, we use one program to create the structural properties of a part and a second program to create the style properties instead of using a single program to create the entire part. In this way, we can use a cabinet design software package to develop the basic product structure and then add styling features to finish the design.

The styling programs can be developed using any of the programming techniques described earlier in this section. We envision that every part has a structural program. Certain parts will also have a style program associated with it. In those cases, the style program is run after the structural program.

Some parts have two structural programs, one for the front side and one for the back side. In these cases, each structural program also has a style program associated with it.

Each style program also has display geometry data associated with it. This data can be read by the design program and used to display the style features on the design as it is being developed. This means that, for the entire system to work, the system used to create the style program must also create the display data.

The final result is an easy to use but powerful system for creating furniture fabrication programs. It allows individual furniture pieces to be designed at a computer terminal where not only the structure, but also the styling of the piece can be examined. It offers virtually unlimited styling flexibility without requiring styling program support from the software supplier.

As this is being written, this system is in the formative stages. By the time you read this, it certainly should have evolved. I believe that this offers a starting point and that from this start, the technology will improve and expand so that creating programs for furniture fabrication will become fast, easy and flexible.

This programming area will likely grow rapidly. Kitchen cabinets have been the first successful commercial application of product, rather than part programming. I have seen systems in Europe for automatically designing and building complex staircases. As furniture fabrication becomes more accepted, systems to generate the necessary programs automatically for almost any type of furniture will also become available. The ideas that I have just expressed could form the basis for these systems. Who knows, after all this talk about program generation, it is possible that program generation for furniture fabrication will become almost totally automatic in the near future.

Because of the limits of a book of this type, I have only offered an overview of programming. What I have explained are the fundamentals. Advances are occurring every year and new, easier, faster programming systems keep coming. Advances in the last ten years have been nothing short of incredible. CAD systems that cost millions of dollars can now be purchased for under $20,000 and the new systems work better. Programs that used to take weeks to perfect can now be generated in minutes using a programming probe. It is likely that the fundamentals I have presented won't change much. What will change is that simpler and faster methods will become available.

One final caution about advancing technology. Make certain that the company you purchase your CAD/CAM system and CNC router from have a policy of offering system upgrades rather than requiring you to scrap your investment and buy a new machine or package to get new features and technology.

One thing you can be sure of is that these technologies will continue to advance. Don't lock yourself into a system where you can't continuously advance with advancing technology. These systems should be purchased to make your company competitive. To remain competitive you can't allow your competition to buy capabilities that you can't easily add to the systems you rely on every day.

# Chapter 9

## Your People - The Key to Success

# Chapter 9

## Your People - The Key to Success

Furniture Fabrication differs from traditional furniture manufacturing in another major way. Productivity and success in furniture fabrication depends on the attitude and efforts of your people to a larger degree than most of us are used to.

There are a lot of jobs in a furniture plant today where the attitude of the employee has little effect on job performance. If you are removing parts, every five seconds from a machine, it doesn't particularly matter if you like your job and the company or not. You still have to remove a part every five seconds and your output, and its effect on the company, will be no different if you are happy or miserable.

Most companies try and maintain the best possible employee morale, but are not willing to invest real money into employee attitude because, in the long run, it will make little difference.

Furniture fabrication is quite a different situation, however. Employee attitudes will have a substantial impact on both productivity and profits. Each cell is almost a company of its own. Because of that, I believe that along with a new manufacturing system must also come changes in traditional management practices.

This chapter is a departure from my normal engineering and technical writings. In this chapter, I will offer some concepts and ideas on the people aspects of running a manufacturing company.

The management approach and practices that I will present in this chapter did not just happen one day. They have been collected over many years from what I believe is a very unique perspective.

A few years ago, these ideas were rather unique and I was aware of no other company that was either aware of or using them. Today, however, I have found that many high-technology companies have evolved and embraced many, if not most of these concepts. I believe that this is a case where the next step is a matter of evolution that occurs to many people at the same time.

It is important to understand, whether or not you agree with the approaches that I present, that a new management style is needed if you hope to compete in the New World. The management style itself offers a competitive advantage that is difficult to compete with.

My company builds rather expensive, high-technology machine tools. These are sold to companies of all sizes to help them modernize their factory production methods.

Selling these products involves getting to know our customer very well. We must fully understand their methods, goals and technical capability. To be successful in selling the product, however, we were required to probe much deeper. It was necessary that we understand our customers as people. We had to determine their desires and fears. We had to understand the corporate politics within their organization.

As I said, the products we sold were expensive and so we normally dealt with the CEO or other high officials within the company. With smaller companies, the purchase of our machine might be the largest capital expenditure the company ever made. In larger companies, the engineer or manager that was purchasing the machine was likely betting his or her career on the outcome.

This has offered us a unique perspective. Not only could we judge the effectiveness of different programs and management attitudes in our own company, but we could also see their effectiveness in thousands of diverse companies with which we had contact.

It is from this perspective that I offer this chapter.

"Without good people it will be virtually impossible for you to be successful". You have heard and read this before and I agree totally. It is true.

The inverse, however is not true. That is, if you have good people you will be successful. Good people will generally result in a company that survives, but not necessarily prospers. I believe to compete on a worldwide scale today requires good people but also requires a proper motivating structure. To try and understand what I mean by a "proper motivating structure", we are going to divert for a little while.

Communism is a political and economic system based on the state. People are to produce according to their ability and, for the benefit of the state and society in general. People exist to serve the state and the state has the responsibility to take care of the people according to their needs. It operates under rules or laws, which are established by the leaders of the state, and these rules, along with people's responsibility, change as needed. There are no inalienable rights to which people are entitled, other than those that are given by the state for the benefit of all.

This entire economic structure operates under central control. Leaders decide where resources are to be directed, what is to be produced, how much people are to be paid and generally how things are to be done. People are to put aside their own personal greed and are to be motivated by a desire to serve the state and help everyone to live a better life. They are expected to trust the state and its leaders to do what is best for them. They are to be motivated, not by their own greed, but by a desire to enhance the common good.

The wealth that is created by this effort is shared by all rather than hoarded by a few rich individuals accumulating vast wealth while masses live in poverty. There is no wealthy privileged class to take advantage of the common workers. Total economic failure by an individual just doesn't happen. Everyone is taken care of.

This economic theory actually has some appealing points, especially if you are one of the workers who doesn't have anything. In fact, it might even be to your own personal benefit. And, herein lies the problem.

People ARE, in fact, worried about their own personal interests. It is against human nature to put the state, the government or any other group of people ahead of your own personal interest. Survival is a basic instinct. Your economic well being is rooted in that instinct. The idea that you must rise above these base instincts for the common good might sound good, but it just doesn't work. And that is the problem with this whole communistic economic system. It just doesn't work. History has shown that Communism is a failed economic system. It has failed in a spectacular way in the Solviet Union, and I believe it will either change or fail in other areas of the world where it is still followed, simply because it goes against basic human nature.

If you have followed me to this point and you agree, here is something to think about. Almost every company in the U.S., and especially the larger companies, are run using this same failed communist economic system. And if that is not enough, it doesn't work any better for a company than it does for a country.

In these companies, people are hired and encouraged to work for the betterment of the company. If the company is successful, they will take care of you. All activities of the company are directed from above through a bureaucracy very similar to the political bureaucracy in a communistic country. In the company, any rights you have are not necessarily due you but instead are rights given to you by the company, and those rights, and the work rules, are directed from above and can be changed as needed. You certainly have the ability to advance, but not necessarily by doing the best job possible but instead by pleasing the bureaucrats above you in the company. Most jobs are rigidly defined little boxes with little room for individual achievement. People squeeze into their little boxes, do the tasks that are prescribed, go home and complain about their day and then get up and do it again. When you think about it, it really doesn't work here any better than it did in Russia.

If this structure doesn't work, why is everyone using it? Simple, they don't know it doesn't work. For decades in Russia, the Russian people believed that their standard of living was as good as, or better than, the rest of the world. Certainly in those areas where the Russians were measured against others; sports, the arts, etc, they either dominated or did very well. Just as Russia dominates the rest of the world in sports, the Russian economy must also dominate economies in the rest of the world. Just imagine the shock and disappointment when the Russian people found this just wasn't true.

Companies don't realize how poorly their overall structure works simply because everyone they compete against uses the same structure. They will quickly find that their system is lacking, as soon as they are forced to compete against a company that uses a better overall system. If you can develop this better system, just imagine the competitive advantage it could offer you.

Now let's look at the capitalistic, free market system. We are looking at an economic, rather than a political system so we are interested in the economic free market rather than the representative democratic political system. The economic system and the political system are tied together somewhat, however, they are not the same thing. In a free market system, first and foremost there is a set of fundamental, inalienable rights that each person has. These rights are something that belong to each person equally, simply because they are alive, and are not rights given to them by the government. In fact, in a capitalistic, democratic free market system, such as that in the U.S., the government gets its power from the people rather than the other way around. The government is "of the people, by the people and for the people." The government is there to maintain order and justice and serve the people. The people are not there to serve the government.

Plans, decisions and the overall operation of the marketplace is not controlled by a central planning group, but instead is comprised of millions of decisions by millions of people in pursuit of their own well-being. Prosperity and the accumulation of wealth reward good decisions. Losses and possibly poverty punish poor decisions. In this system it is possible to succeed beyond your wildest dreams. It is also possible to fail, utterly.

Overall the system works like natural selection in nature. Those traits and actions that benefit the economy and society are incorporated into our daily lives and those efforts that fall short are simply discarded. The fit survive and the unfit and weak perish. It's a brutal world, this capitalism. This natural selection system however, over millions of years in nature has improved all species allowing them to adapt to a changing environment. It has brought man to our current position. At the same time it has eliminated well over 95% of all species that have ever existed. Nature eliminates you when you can not adapt. Capitalism does much the same thing.

I'm not here to pass judgement as to whether this is good or bad. It simply is, and it works. It works in nature and it works in economic systems. This is the core of capitalism and the result is good. The overall standard of living in capitalistic countries is higher, often much higher, than the overall plight of people in countries following communist economic ideas. Perhaps they have lofty ideals, but following those lofty ideals results in everyone suffering.

In capitalism, each person tries to take care of themselves and their families. Each company tries to take care of itself. Everyone is trying to make more profit by doing things better than everyone else does. When they find better ways to do things they are rewarded with more profit. Others must then find an even better method and the cycle continues.

The overall result, not the purpose of all the effort, but the result, is that the overall economy benefits. Things are getting better. They are not getting better because anyone is trying to make the economy better. They are simply trying to make more money for themselves. The fact that their efforts to make more money actually help the economy and everyone in the economy is a by-product, and not the purpose, of the efforts. People are doing what comes naturally, they are following their instinct for survival and in the process, the standard of living of all of society is improving.

In this part of the book, I am going to suggest that you incorporate a capitalistic structure for your new furniture fabrication company in place of the communistic ideas that are currently being used to run companies. It is possible to structure your company to take advantage of this natural, driving force in your employees. It is possible to structure the company so that the employees work, not for the good of the company but for their own profit and benefit. In doing so, they will benefit the company, management, the shareholders and the other employees as a by-product of their efforts.

When tapped in this manner, your employees can make your company so incredibly powerful and competitive that dominating a market becomes almost easy. When a company is structured in this manner, it takes almost no effort to run it. Set up the structure, help define the goals and let the company run.

You have likely heard that the vast majority of new jobs are created by small business. Have you ever noticed that a small business can perform all the functions needed with very few people while a large business requires substantially more people to perform the same functions. I have also noticed that small businesses tend to operate with a bit more harmony. As the business size increases, corporate politics emerge. As the size of a company gets larger, politics assume a larger and larger role. When the company is small, it is naturally capitalistic. As it grows it becomes more centralized and more communistic in it management structure and policies.

I am going to propose something that I believe holds a key to getting substantially more from each of your people and to making your company incredibly strong and flexible.

To thrive in a highly competitive market requires that each of your people dominate their counterparts in your competitors companies. Taking normal people, placing them in normal corporate structures will get you normal results. To dominate your market you must do better.

Before we continue, lets talk about attitude. Attitude alone won't solve your problem, however, the wrong attitude will prevent you from ever solving your problem regardless of what else you do. Now a surprise. When I talk about attitude, I am not talking about the attitude of your people. I am talking about your attitude toward your people.

The accountants and money counters in many companies sow the seeds that eventually grow to either limit or eventually destroy the company. They convince management that labor is a cost.

Labor IS a cost, isn't it? Actually, this is the traditional way of looking at labor.

During the industrial revolution, labor was viewed as another ingredient of production just as the building, machinery and utilities. It was a cost to be controlled, reduced and kept in check. An overzealous campaign to get as much as possible for as little as possible forced labor to organize into unions to try and protect themselves. A basic conflict then emerged. Laborers trying to get as much as possible for themselves and management trying to keep labor costs down. This basic attitude exists yet today, however, I don't believe it exists to quite the level it did in the past.

The fact that it does exist can be seen in the announcements that such and such a company is closing its US plant and moving to some less developed country where labor is cheap. Obviously, labor is viewed as a major expense.

Why do I think that this attitude is not as prevalent as in the past? I base this belief on two things. First, union membership has been steadily falling. At one time about one third of this nation's workers were members of a labor union. Today that number has fallen to under 10%. It appears to me that fewer workers feel the need to be represented by a union. They must feel reasonably secure without outside representation. The second reason may actually contribute to the first.

The idea that labor is just another resource which should be purchased at the lowest cost relies on the fact that there is more labor available than is required. Today, that is becoming less valid. Labor is becoming more difficult to obtain and most people with any marketable skill can move to another job with another company with little difficulty.

Management must satisfy workers if they intend to remain in business. Today, there is much more effort spent in trying to create a compensation package than at any time in history. The conflict within management is incredible. Management must provide good jobs at good wages with competitive fringe benefits but, labor is a cost so we must try and keep everything as low as possible. What a balancing act!

If you view labor as an expense and workers as people you must pay enough to keep but not one dime more, you are establishing a corporate attitude that will make it much more difficult for you to ever compete in a worldwide market. Just as your product and marketing must be much better than your competitors, your product costs must also be lower.

Yes, but doesn't lower cost labor result in lower cost products? In general, yes, but its not good enough. The amount you save by holding down your workers pay will not give you enough savings to create a competitive advantage. You have to save a lot more. I promise you that if you cut your workers pay in half to try and get enough savings to make a difference, they will all leave. Traditional methods and traditional thinking are not going to work here. We are going to have to define a different structure and a different method of working with your people to get the results we want. This is where attitude and the idea of capitalism in a company becomes important.

First, some observations. Small companies are more efficient than large ones. We have already touched on this but I repeat it here because this simple observation holds the key to making your company cost competitive. Most small companies are started by a group of people, working together, trying to survive and prosper. As employees are hired, they become part of the family. Everyone realizes that their future depends on the success or failure of the company. Everyone knows that their contribution will have a direct effect on the success or failure of the company and, on their own success or failure. There is a lot to be done and not many rules about how to do it. As the company becomes more successful, those few who were part of the start-up will generally prosper as they take over the more responsible positions and new people are hired. The new people will feel a bit less connected to the company than the original pioneers. They will generally feel that they have less impact on the profit or loss of the company. They will also feel a bit more secure than the original people because the company is successful, expanding and will take care of them. They won't realize just how shaky the whole venture is, at least they won't know this as well as those who started at ground zero.

Now the company is starting to grow for real. It must be expanded. More people are hired. We now need some "professionals". We hire an accountant to track the money and expenses. We hire a manager to run the factory. We can't keep running using the "seat of the pants" approach. We must get more professional. We develop job descriptions for management and labor. It is taking more and more people to keep the place running.

Costs are creeping up. It's hard to believe, but, with all the volume, the cost of each item produced is rising and profit margins are shrinking. We need to cut costs. We could eliminate a layer of middle management and slightly reduce direct labor cost and possibly get through.

The middle management move was pretty tough. Some of those folks have been around for awhile. The workers were not happy about the wage cut but they have to understand.

It isn't working. Although costs are down, so is productivity. We aren't producing as many products and the cost per unit is still increasing. Even with the lower overhead that resulted from the management cuts, we are starting to lose money. We can't tolerate this. We have never had a price increase and everyone around us has been increasing prices. It is time for a nominal, but necessary price increase. It's really the only way out of this mess.

Oh gee!! sales are off. We are going to have to pare this thing down and lay off some more people. We need to match the production rate to the lower sales rate. At this rate, we will also need to let some more management go so that we can cover the overhead at the new, lower production rate. This might be a good time for some special promotions and sales programs to get the sales rate back up. Nobody seems very happy and some of our really good folks have left for better jobs with other companies.

The lower production level has resulted in higher costs even with the reduced labor expense. Overhead costs have dropped but the cost of the new sales program has more than used up those savings. We are losing money at an alarming rate. The only way to survive is to raise prices. You know the rest of the story.

There is a point in flying an airplane where you are slow with the nose pointed up. The drag caused by this attitude is so high that regardless of how much power you apply, you continue to descend. Even at full power, the plane slowly sinks. Pilots call this being on the "back side of the power curve". This company is on the "back side of the power curve".

The reactive thinking that caused the above situation will cause the company to fail if it doesn't change. Conventional wisdom says that you need to replace top management with a new crew and new thinking. You don't necessarily need a new crew but you do need new thinking. At no time during this entire episode did anyone ever stop to try and analyze what was really happening. The corporate structure evolved from something that worked into something that didn't work. The evolution seemed normal. At no time during the change did it appear that anyone was doing anything wrong. That is because no one was actually DOING anything. Things were happening to them, they were not making things happen. It is difficult to take a critical look at something that is working.

The biggest problem with the above scenario is the attitude. The attitude that developed, although common in American business, is very destructive. To try and understand this, let's go back to basics.

Your company is people. You absolutely must keep this in mind. As the company grew, you installed "professional" systems, not to help the people but to help you structure and control the people. You were moving from a capitalistic approach to management to a totalitarian dictatorship. As an example, let's talk about job descriptions.

Job descriptions are devices used in large companies to make certain that all of the necessary functions are completed and that each job works with, and interacts with the others. This is a vital step if you intend to minutely control each and every person in the company. One way to look at a job description is to think of it as a box containing all of the responsibilities and duties of the person holding the job.

**Job Description**

These job descriptions can then be stacked next to one another to provide a nice neat little corporate structure with no gaps and no overlap as such:

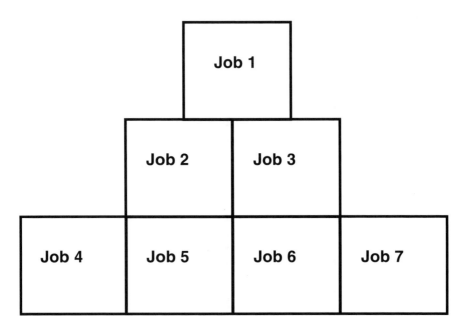

This is a nice, neat, orderly corporate structure. It is the way that most companies are structured. In larger companies there are likely hundreds or maybe thousands of boxes instead of just seven. Now, lets look at the people that are to fit in these boxes. Each person has a unique set of capabilities, talents and limitations. They are not simple squares like the jobs. Instead, they are indefinite curved shapes like this:

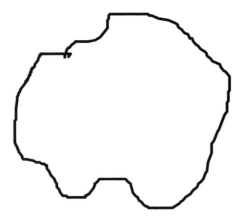

Now, let's put the person into the job.

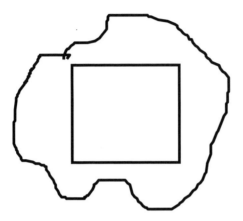

As you can see, this person is capable of doing this job. The entire job is covered and there are no gaps. In industry today this is considered a good fit. This person would be considered a good employee and would likely be very successful in their job.

What about the part of the person overhanging the job box? That is talent and capability that the person has but that the job doesn't require. That is unused potential. What will it be used for in this job? Since the actual job doesn't require it, it will likely be used to try and better the person in other ways than doing a good job. It will be used to maneuver within corporate politics. If each of the job boxes are filled in a like manner, there is an incredible amount of energy available for corporate politics and individual maneuvering. In fact, if you analyze the above drawing you will find that there is as much talent and energy available for empire building and political maneuvering as there is for actually doing the job. I can see where this can be a problem. Let's try the most obvious solution, make the job bigger. Increase the job requirements to use more of the available talent of the employee. In other words, make the job box bigger. Here is the result.

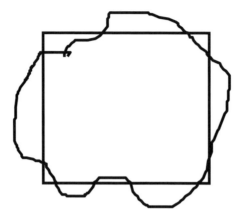

Now we have a new problem. Some parts of the job aren't being done. There are gaps where the person's capability, talents and energy just don't cover the job. Maybe we can train the person in those areas and give them the extra needed capability. The next person, however, will have a different shape. They will fit the box differently and will require different training to fit. A different training program for each person is just not going to be practical and who will do the job areas the person can't do while he or she is being trained? Better to make the boxes smaller so that everyone fits well. Unfortunately, this is the attitude of most larger businesses.

The point I am trying to make is that the overall attitude that leads to workers being regarded as an expense and workers being forced into little job boxes is flawed. Fundamentally, the overall approach is wrong or at least it doesn't work very well.

So what is the answer? How do your reconcile the needs of the company for structure and control with the reality of the people working for the company. Let us go back and see how the little company operated when it was actually working well. First, there were no job boxes. There were no job descriptions. Each person was hired to handle some general area. This area may not have been very well defined. They were each given a job title and this told everybody which area they were to work in. If we were to look at the structure it would look something like this:

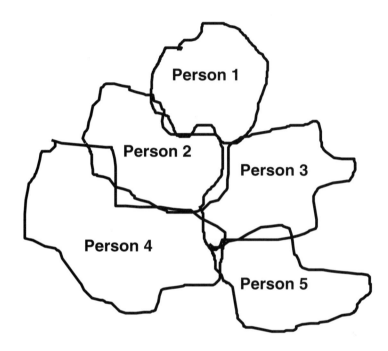

There are several things to notice. First, almost the entire capability of each person is being used. Because of this, it takes fewer people to get all the jobs done. There are some areas where people overlap. These are areas of potential conflict. There are also areas that nobody covers.

In this informal structure, there is not much structure. The work that needs to be done is matched to the people available to do the work. The job and the people available are the major factors. Individual job structures are not formally defined but are whatever is necessary to reach the overall goals. There is not much potential for corporate politics or job maneuvering. Virtually all the effort is required just to get the job done.

The key concept here is that the goal or the job to be done and the people and their talents are the major factors to be considered. The job structure is totally flexible. It changes to match the reality of the people in each job. The job structure and the overall structure of the company itself is rather unimportant.

Let's say, in the above company, Person 2 quit. This leaves a hole in the organization as shown below.

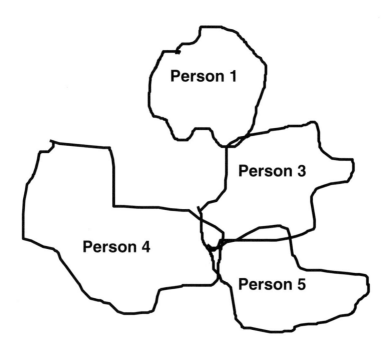

We will now add a New Person 2 to the organization. Notice that the New Person 2 does not have the same shape as the old one. Also notice that the organization has shifted to accommodate the new person.

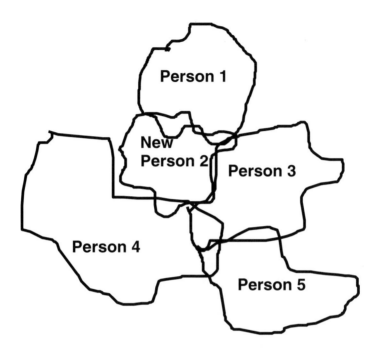

The job for the new Person 2 is different than the job for the original Person 2 even though the job title may be the same. In the real world, not only does the job change to accommodate different people but the shape of each person's capability also change over time, which also affects the job. In reality, people will grow into the open areas between jobs to fill in the real needs. Areas of overlap will become areas of conflict and in a healthy, growing company these areas will be resolved defining the job boundary somewhere between the two people.

To the traditional business manager this looks like a totally unmanageable business structure. I assure you that is not the case. A company can be managed using this structure and, in fact, it will operate much more efficiently and produce product at a much lower cost than the traditional structure. How do you adjust the jobs on an ongoing basis? You don't. This type of structure cannot be micro-managed. It is not possible for a manager or group of managers to control what their people do.

This type of business structure puts faith, real faith in the ability and motivation of the people. It also relies heavily on an individual motivation program that we will talk about in a minute. It requires the proper management attitude. That brings us full circle back to attitude. It is finally time to address management attitude directly.

There are essentially three groups of people that make up the company and a fourth group that is directly affected by the company. The company is made up of shareholders, management and workers. Shareholders are the actual owners of the company. These are the people who provided the money needed to get the company going. They invested their money in hopes that the company could live up to its promise, become successful and in doing so provide them with a return, or profit on their investment.

Management are those who traditionally make the decisions and run the company. I include in management the board of directors, although the board may also be made up of shareholders. Management also includes the top operating, finance and sales people. In fact, management will generally include everyone that has other people reporting to them. Management is the group that is charged with making the company work. They want the company to be successful. They want the company to make a lot of money so that they can receive as much of that money as possible in the form of salary and bonus.

Workers are the people that actually do each of the detail jobs needed to produce the product. They do what management tells them and hope that these decisions are correct. They want the company to be successful so that they are not laid off and they want as high a paycheck as possible in the mean time.

The fourth group that relies on the company are the suppliers, vendors and service people. They are not actually part of the company, although I believe that the company does have real obligations toward its suppliers and vendors.

The company is actually made up of the first three groups. The company is not the shareholders and management who then hire the workers who are a production cost like the machines and materials. This is the most common basic attitude in industry today, however, this attitude, in my opinion will not work in the future business environment in the U.S. This attitude might continue in low labor cost third-world countries for awhile, but will eventually be replaced there also.  The workers are as big a part of the company as the shareholders and management. I believe the company exists to serve those three groups. Each has a vested interest in the company. Each has wagered something very important to them on the success of the company. Shareholders have wagered their investment capital. Management has wagered their careers and the workers have wagered their futures and bet their family income and security on the company. In return, I believe the company owes each of these groups. Just as with a capitalist country like the United States, the company exists for the people not the other way around.

To be really successful, especially in a highly competitive market you absolutely must have full efforts of all three groups. You will only get that effort if all groups firmly feel and believe that they are an integral part of the company. They must also feel that management recognizes that they are an important and essential component of that company. It is also essential that they believe that if the company is successful they will be successful, if the company does poorly they will do poorly and if the company fails they will fail. Management recognizes that their future is directly tied to the success or failure of the company. Shareholders also know that they will only get rewards if the company is successful. The workers, however, don't normally share this belief. They all believe that they will fail if the company fails. Few also believe that they will directly benefit if the company is successful. They will be paid their normal wage regardless of whether the company is doing well or poorly, within limits of course. This is an important point that must be addressed in most companies or the full potential of the organization will not be realized.

The core philosophy for running a capitalistic company is that if the company is successful, each of the groups should be successful. If the company is not successful, each of the groups should be equally unsuccessful. The company is a boat and everyone in the company is in that boat. If the boat progresses, everyone in it should also progress. Many companies are run as if management and the shareholder are in the boat but the workers are swimming along side. They are helping push the boat along but if one gets left behind once in awhile, well, that's business. This attitude actually worked for many years but, today, business is so much more competitive that a company that runs using this approach will be lucky to remain in their market. They will certainly not dominate it and if they currently do, they are highly vulnerable to a modern thinking company. If you cannot get all three groups focused on moving your company forward you cannot possibly be competitive enough to prosper in the New World.

The core attitude about how everyone fits into the company must come from the top. This attitude must be a basic belief and it must provide a guiding principal for everything that is done.

Now we must tie each of the groups to the success of the company. There are as many ways of doing this as there are companies. I favor using simple cash. I am a strong believer in bonus systems and, over the years I have tried almost every type of bonus plan you can think of.

A properly structured bonus program is the key concept that will allow your company to operate more like a capitalistic country. Structure your compensation program so that as the company becomes more successful, each employee becomes more successful individually. Then, openly focus on increasing each person's pay as the primary goal. That's right, don't worry about the company. Focus on making the people's pay as high as possible. If you have structured the pay plans correctly, the company will prosper as a by-product of increasing people's pay.

You will be shocked at how much concern and effort people are willing to put out when working in this type of structure. Decision making becomes very clear, with little effort going into anything but increasing their own pay. The innovations, insight and efficiency of an organization motivated in this manner will provide a level of competitiveness that companies run the old way can't possibly compete with.

Now, the bad news. A properly structured bonus program will cause people to take an interest in everything. Management will no longer be able to make decisions without explaining, justifying and obtaining a consensus. After all, these decisions are directly affecting people's pay so they feel they have a right to influence those decisions. Harnessed properly, this can be a powerful driving force resulting in better decisions and a much more competitive company. It can also be a highly destructive force if management refuses to share decision making with essentially everybody.

I can think of one example where this caused the plan to fail. A manufacturing company installed a profit bonus plan. As I predicted, after a couple of checks, people started to take an interest in anything that affected profits.

Then the president of that company decided to add some attractive landscaping to a new plant expansion. As you would expect, he received much criticism about spending money foolishly. Unwilling to give up the right to do whatever he wanted, the president gave everyone a small raise and cancelled the plan.

Just as with countries, you can not have dictator power in a capitalistic corporation. If you want to tap into the consensus you have to allow them to encroach on management areas that traditionally are reserved for top management. This doesn't mean that you can't purchase landscaping for your new expansion. It simply means that you have to sell the idea to your people.

The first thing you must realize is that most employees do not understand the impact that this kind of expenditure will have on their pay. They think that the entire expense will be immediately subtracted from profits. In fact, most expenses must be capitalized and then depreciated over several years. The positive image the more attractive factory presents to customers and vendors is balanced by a rather insignificant change in profit bonus. In fact, you could argue that the more successful image would attract more business and the profits might actually increase.

Obviously, this is an extra step, but this extra step encourages discussion of factors that affect the company as well as educating the employees as to how the finance and accounting systems work. These will have a positive overall impact. This process can also keep you from making a serious error.

Because you must explain, discuss and justify planned actions with your people, you are forced to view the plan from many different perspectives. From these views, sometimes the plan cannot stand up. I have experienced many instances where actions that I proposed were not implemented because in the ensuing discussion either flaws were uncovered or my perspective was changed.

A properly working bonus plan is the key to a capitalistic corporation. It will focus people on everything that affect profit and profits will rise. The biggest change will be with management who no longer run things, but instead manage the collective opinion. If you can accept this change, the rewards can be great.

There is a caution, however. It is very easy for a bonus plan to have more of a negative impact than a positive one. You must take into account human nature when structuring a bonus plan. The easiest way to generate a negative response is to provide a surprise bonus. Things are going well, we are making money so lets share some of it with our people. This sounds like a great idea, but my experience shows that it won't work. First, since it wasn't expected and people didn't have time to adjust their minds to the terms or amounts, the actual payout and amounts won't be regarded as fair. The most common attitude is that it was an awful small amount compared to the effort it took to actually generate the profit. It is not uncommon for some people to actually quit their jobs after receiving a surprise bonus.

This phenomenon is very common with first line production supervision. A foreman or supervisor is doing an outstanding job. The regular pay review isn't going to occur for six months or so and you want to show that you appreciate them. A small extra boost in pay will, more times than not cause them to quit. They know that they are doing a good job and they believe that the job they are doing is worth a great deal to the company. When the company responds with a very small reward, they feel that they have been slighted. It minimizes the effort they have been putting in and makes them feel that the company doesn't really appreciate their efforts. This certainly wasn't the intent of your actions, but the results were negative nonetheless.

Recently I talked with a middle management employee of a large company. Her company had just declared a surprise bonus, the first ever. She had received 2 ½ % and was complaining that top management received 10%. Feelings were very negative and it was very clear to me that, at least in her case, the company would have been much better off not offering a bonus at all. I believe that this same bonus, structured ahead of time, with top management receiving 10% and middle management receiving 2 ½% would have had a totally different impact. These types of programs must be sold.

The logic behind bonus distribution must be discussed and since no bonus has ever been paid, these ideas can be sold and accepted. Once we are over that hurdle, the actual pay out should be a positive event. Money makes people emotional. If they have to deal with both the money and the concept of the bonus plan at the same time the chances of success are reduced. If they can deal with the concepts behind the bonus first, without actual money being involved they will generally be much more positive. Once events occur and the bonus actually gets paid there is a much better chance that the whole thing will be viewed as a positive which helps motivate the employee.

A bonus is a tool used to focus people, encourage cooperation and strive for a goal. A bonus which occurs after the fact, cannot accomplish any of these proposes. A bonus that occurs after the fact also has one other very negative effect. When a bonus is defined, goals are reached and rewards received, the employee feels that they have earned the extra money. They also feel that it occurred, at least partially, because of their efforts. It is normal for them to feel that they controlled or influenced the outcome. When you provide a surprise bonus it is clear that you, and only you, controlled the outcome. You, and not the employee control their fate. Their income depends on your good will. This makes people uncomfortable. I call the thinking behind this type of action "plantation mentality". "After all I have done for you, why don't you appreciate me?" Nobody likes to be a slave subject to the whims of a superior regardless of how well they live.

When you develop a bonus plan, try and understand how the people operating under the plan will feel. Try and imagine yourself in their place. A bonus plan is more than money. The bonus is a complete reward system for reaching certain goals. This includes defining the goal, working toward the goal and then being compensated for reaching the goal. All aspects of this reward system are important. If you shortcut the system, for example providing a bonus after the fact, you eliminate some of the steps. In this case, the goal wasn't defined and therefore it also wasn't reached. At least in the minds of the people it wasn't earned. In this case, the bonus is nothing more than a gift from an all-powerful master.

It is very important that top management be part of the team and not master of the team. To accomplish this requires that you give up total "after the fact" power to control pay and substitute plans and programs defined ahead of time where the employee feels that they, and not you, control how much money they make. Management still controls these expenses but they do it through planned programs not through gifts. It is like a great banquet. Employees would like to dine with management at the same time, as a team. They don't want to be served the leftovers after management has finished eating.

Over the years, my experience with a variety of bonus programs has created three guiding principals for an employee bonus. These principals have proved successful each time I have used them and I believe they will work for most companies.

The bonus must be substantial enough to get attention.
There must be no limit.
The bonus must be based on objective measurement that the employee has major control or influence over.

Let's look at each point, one at a time.

What is substantial? If 100% of your pay is based on bonus, I believe that is substantial. Will people work this way? Generally, no, although there are some notable exceptions. Many salesmen work on a commission-only arrangement. These people are generally very motivated but it does require a special type of person to work this way. I worked for years on a bonus only salary arrangement. It was based on a percentage of the profits that the company made and at the time it was established the company wasn't making any money. Under this plan the company became quite profitable. This type of pay plan, although not practical for most situations, does result in a real commitment and a focus on profits.

For most people, a bonus-only pay program results in too high a level of insecurity. Despite this fact, I believe that the bonus should be a significant part of the overall pay plan and that it should be the difference between a barely adequate salary and really good pay. For management, the general method which has worked best for me is to provide a base pay well under their counterparts in other similar companies and then a bonus which, if things are going very well, will result in an overall salary and bonus well above their counterparts. A bonus, which accounts for a half to two thirds of total take-home pay, provides a huge incentive. It has also been my experience that this level of bonus is practical and does generate a strong drive for profits.

There is one potentially negative effect of this type of compensation plan, however, I personally consider it more of a positive than a negative. Many really talented managers won't work under this type of plan. It takes someone with a special set of personality traits to function this way. The person that will work this way is an adventurer, a pioneer. They are generally optimistic with a very positive attitude and a can-do approach to almost any challenge. This will eliminate a large number of really good managers who aren't quite so optimistic and simply don't want to risk their pay on the fates of the business world. I find, however, that the type of person that will work under this type of pay plan is exactly the type of person that I want working for me. I have no real proof but I believe that this type of person makes a better competitor and will make your company stronger.

There are some real advantages to a heavily bonus based pay plan. First, when you are paying out the big bucks it is because things are going very well and you can generally afford them. When things are going well, employees feel that they deserve more and with this type of plan they are getting more. There is a certain mystique about employees in a highly successful company. Corporate headhunters will be calling your people with attractive offers when things are going well in your company. That is the time when you are paying your people the highest salaries and generally, they will not be particularly interested in leaving when things are going so well and they are making so much money. Also, a plan that accrues the bonus over a period of time and then pays it out each month over a subsequent period of time makes the employee believe that the money is "banked" for them but they must remain employees to actually get it. For example, the bonus for a six month period can be accrued in a bonus pool and then one sixth of the pool is paid out each month for the next six months while a new bonus is accrued. Once they have received the previously accrued bonus, they have accrued a new bonus and so, they feel that any time they leave, they are giving up a substantial pool of money. Make certain that your plan makes it very clear that the employee gives up all claims to the bonus pool should they leave.

Let's say the economy falters and your sales and profits drop. The cost of all of your management also drops. Should you actually lose money, management may take a 50 to 66% CUT in pay. That fact alone will work wonders to keep profits up. This direct tie-in makes your company much more resilient. Won't your people leave if their pay is drastically cut? In poor economic times, few jobs are available. Headhunters won't be seeking people in your company if your company is doing poorly. It doesn't take long for your management to recognize that the easiest way to improve their lot in life is to get your profits back up where they belong. Of course when that happens they are making too much money to change jobs.

I have experienced just how powerful the drive from this type of bonus plan can be. My company had been losing money for several years when we restructured. Bonus programs were put in place, but, since we were not making money anyway, they didn't provide the gut level drive needed. We added a program whereby any month that was a loss would result in an across the board 20% cut in the base pay of all salaried employees the following month. We had one loss month under this program. It never happened again. After years of losses we never even got close to losing money again.

Now understand, when you start digging into peoples pockets this way, they are going to be very unhappy. Normally quiet meek people will aggressively attack anything they believe is keeping the company from making money. To make this program work you must listen to these people. Even better, give the people the power to change those things they feel must be changed to become even more profitable. These programs tap into the very core of people's survival instincts. If you dominate decisions and don't allow the power that's been developed to transform your company, the result will be bitter resentment toward you and toward all top management and the company will likely tear itself apart. If you go with the flow and allow these feelings to manifest themselves as positive improvements the trend will quickly turn and the company will be on the road to record profitability.

The second feature that I believe must be part of any bonus program is that there must be no limit to the amount of money that an employee can make from the bonus. Why? Isn't there a certain point where someone is being paid substantially more then they are worth? Do we have a problem here?

First, no one in your company is being paid what they are worth. It is vital that everyone in the company know and understand this. This is especially true of hourly paid production workers. They are being paid what the job they are doing is worth to the company. This is an important distinction. An example I use often is that if Albert Einstein were hired to cut the grass, he would be paid the rate for job grade one in our company. This is NOT what Albert Einstein is worth, this is what cutting the grass is worth.

Once this distinction between what the person is worth and what the job they are doing is worth is understood and accepted by everyone in your company it will make discussions about pay and bonus rates much easier. It is much more comfortable to discuss how much impact a set of tasks has on the company than to discuss with a person how much impact he or she personally has on the company.

While we are on the subject of pay and attitudes about pay, let's address another major point that hourly paid workers often complain about. You have likely heard people in your company say "what I do is worth more than what they pay me". Of course it is. If it wasn't, the company couldn't pay the overhead and generate a profit and shortly, they will fail and you won't get paid at all. Pay, for everyone, is a balancing act. Your people should understand that the company is trying to pay as much as possible to take care of current people and attract the best people in the future but, they cannot pay so much that the company can't generate a profit, grow and prosper. Balance is the key. People will accept this concept provided they are relatively sure that when things are going well they will share in the success. The bonus program should provide this assurance.

Your people must also understand that under this philosophy, productivity is the key to their future pay. If more product is produced per hour worked, the company can pay a higher rate for each hour and still generate a profit. The company cannot just set any rate of pay that they want. Instead, the company is controlled by the market trying to balance the cost of the products with their desire to pay a good competitive rate to its employees. In the final analysis, the market decides what the employee is paid and the best way to improve that pay is to become more productive.

It is important that all your people know these basic facts. Once they know and accept them, it becomes obvious that the only way to safely get paid more is to make the work you do worth more. Given the correct management atmosphere, this can become the driving force for significant productivity gains. These productivity gains result in lower manufacturing costs which, when passed on to customers in the form of lower prices, result in increased market share.

So, what exactly is the "correct management atmosphere"? Here again, the current philosophy and beliefs in U.S. industry work to derail real progress. There is a core belief that "working hard" is the key to better profits. There are slogans, posters, quality circles, pep talks, discipline procedures, quotas, pay check inserts, productivity seminars and dozens of other programs designed to get your people working harder. I have observed over the years that, pretty much, across the board these have little or no effect on performance. People have a certain basic level of performance which combined with the production "system" provides a certain level of output. The basic level of performance of the people can't really be changed much. On a bad day, it will lag and as part of a major push, it can increase a little, but only for a short period of time. In general, however, it has a certain level of performance and that is the level at which it will operate.

If this is the case, how do you increase productivity? Even more, how do you increase productivity enough to make a real, measurable difference in the marketplace?

Productivity is people working within the system. If you can't really change the performance of the people, then you have to change the system. You must change the basic way your production operates in order to reduce your costs.

W. Edward Deming is an American who is widely credited with teaching the Japanese statistical quality control and principals of management after World War II. Many believe that he is the single biggest factor in the Japanese becoming as successful as they have been over the last several decades. If you are not familiar with his work, I would encourage you to study his philosophy. If you plan to manage anything at all, this will be a great help.

During the last several years, Dr. Deming has conducted seminars for top management of large corporations. One of Dr. Deming's more dramatic exercises in his seminars is conducted with a very large bowl of beads. He mixes 3,200 white beads and 800 red beads. He then established a manufacturing company around the bowl of beads. From the audience he selects people to act as production, management, quality inspection and so forth in the fictitious production company. The production process consists of removing beads from the bowl using a wooden paddle. He uses a paddle that has 50 holes in it. When the paddle is dipped into the bowl, moved around and then withdrawn, it will contain 50 beads, one in each hole. The purpose of this exercise is to produce white beads. Red beads are scrap and must be avoided.

He sets up an incredibly complex production organization. Operation of the paddle is strictly controlled and must be conducted in a very precise manner. There are production training sessions to teach workers how to operate the paddle. He has two inspectors who count the beads and a chief inspector that verifies the count and resolves any discrepancies between the two inspectors.

He spends hours running the "production line". He praises the workers who produce more white beads and threatens those who produce too many red beads. He sets up study groups to study and learn the techniques of those who produce more white beads.

Slogans are developed and posters made to encourage the production of white beads. Failure to produce an adequate number of white beads led to people being disciplined or fired. Production organizations are restructured and people shuffled to try and improve the process. Eventually, then entire plant is threatened with closing if productivity doesn't improve and finally, the whole operation is shut down because of poor performance.

As this demonstration progresses, the audience watches as every method, technique and ploy used by American business is used to try and improve the operation. It is also incredibly clear to the audience that absolutely nothing they do will have any impact at all. The whole exercise makes management look like total fools as they try to influence something they can't influence. It becomes crystal clear that the only possible way to influence the outcome is to change the method of production by reducing the number of red beads or selecting them one at a time, or whatever.

This exercise is designed to demonstrate exactly how a manufacturing business works. It graphically demonstrates that almost all efforts to improve productivity in most factories can't possibly work. Only by focusing on the system rather than the people can you achieve any real improvement.

One other result of Dr. Deming's demonstration highlights another very important point. You will remember that he mixed 3,200 white beads and 800 red beads for a total of 4,000 beads. You would then expect that 20% of the beads selected by the paddle would be red since 20% of the beads in the bowl were red. Thus you assume that the paddle will, over time, select 10 beads out of fifty that are red. This does not happen. In fact, fewer then 20% of the beads turn out to be red and each paddle tends to have a different ratio. How can this be?

One possibility is that red beads are made by painting white beads red. This makes the red beads slightly larger than the white beads and thus can influence the outcome. There may be slight variation in the size of the holes in each paddle, which could also influence the outcome. Regardless of why it happens, this illustrates that there is a natural tendency to make assumptions about your production process without any real evidence to support those assumptions. Managers then make critical decisions based on those false assumptions.

These inaccurate assumptions can have a very negative impact on your operation. It keeps you from properly understanding how things really work. Without understanding exactly how they work, you cannot possibly improve them. It increases complacency and makes you assume that real improvement in certain areas is not possible. If you don't think an area can be improved, you will generally not try and improve it and it won't improve.

The only way to ever know what is really happening in your production operation is to count, track and statistically analyze your operation. Many managers feel this is not important and is something to do only when all else is working properly. Actually, it is a vital step in understanding your operation so that you can get it working properly. It is needed to get your operation working properly and without this understanding you will never really make progress in improving your productivity. If you wait for everything to work before you begin this process, it will likely never get working correctly.

My recommendation is that you assume that neither you, nor any of your people really know how things work. This belief should be widespread and accepted by the entire organization. Since you don't know how things really work, you and your people should conduct an ongoing effort to try and figure it out. It is very important that you constantly question every aspect of the production operation. Your current understanding and belief should be labeled as "our current beliefs" indicating that they may be wrong.

Many people in an organization get a great deal of security by understanding and accepting the way things are. This approach takes that security away from them. They must get their security from belonging to an organization that is constantly seeking the true nature of things and one that does not expect its members to have all the answers. There must be no stigma associated with discovering that basic assumptions are wrong. In fact, employees who discover the true nature of the operation should be praised and finding an error in management's understanding of the operation should be somewhat like finding a gold nugget in a mountain stream. It should be an event that is celebrated and the organization should be encouraged to constantly try and better understand.

Let's return to the question of paying someone too much as part of a bonus program. The key to the bonus atmosphere is that the employee feels that they can earn substantially more than their counterparts in other companies. You want extraordinary effort and commitment to the company. For that you must offer extraordinary personal financial potential.

The bonus should be structured so that as the employee makes more and more money, the company also makes more and more money. If the company is benefiting substantially from the employees efforts why should the employee not share in the success? The only way to rationalize reducing the employee's reward is that you can hire someone qualified to replace the employee for half or less of what you are paying your current employee. This totally ignores the fact that it was the promise of future rewards that drove the employee to achieve the success you are now enjoying. Will the replacement have the same drive for success?

Remember the fairy tale of the goose that laid golden eggs? A company that is thriving and prospering is just such an animal. As the company enjoys corporate success, if you try and take personal success from those who made it happen you are killing the goose. In my opinion, in a properly structured bonus program you want your employee to make as much money as possible. That means that you are becoming more successful. Once the program is in place the stated goal of both you and your people is to increase their pay as high as possible. You must work together toward that goal. People will put forth incredible effort for a team whose goal is making them more money.

There will be times where extra profit for the company comes into conflict with extra bonus for the people. To maintain the proper attitude among the people it is vital that these decisions be made in favor of more bonus for the people. It is difficult to convince people that your goal is higher bonuses for the people if you opt for lower bonuses and higher profits whenever a decision must be made.

An example of this is a bonus based on achieving a certain level of profit. If the actual profit is right at that level, any good accountant can make it fall on one side or the other all within "Generally Accepted Accounting Practices". Should this occur, make sure you reach the goal. The amounts associated with this decision are very small when viewed in total, however the employee attitudes generated are very significant. Again, I state what I believe to be the heart of a bonus plan. Employees must feel that top management's goal is to pay them as much as possible while maintaining a strong healthy company.

There should be no limit to the size of the bonus. At least within the structure of the bonus program there should be no limit. There will always be a practical limit based on the maximum that can be sold, produced or shipped. The limit, however, should come from the marketplace and not from the bonus program.

A program that pays a bonus to a certain point, and then either stops it, or substantially reduces it, tells the employee that there is the limit. That limit is all you want from them. There is little incentive to work for a higher level. In fact, as you approach the limit, it might make sense to ease up a little anyway so you don't shoot past the limit. You certainly don't want to waste good business at the lower bonus level. It is better to save the business for next year when the higher base bonus is in effect.

If you put a limit on your bonus, you are effectively putting a limit on your potential. You are not saving the extra bonus on those higher levels of business but are instead assuring yourself that you will never reach those higher levels.

A better way to handle the situation is to determine the absolute most that could possibly be achieved under the plan and then double the bonus for anything achieved above that level. There is little risk in that plan since you don't believe you can achieve that level anyway. Should you actually achieve that level, the extra bonus you pay out will be small indeed, compared to the extraordinary level of success you achieved.

This type of plan drives people from the inside, from day one. As they become more successful and get closer to the goal, they increase, not decrease their efforts. You will be surprised at how often this achieves results well beyond the limits you though possible. When you focus the real enthusiasm and drive of your people toward a clear goal the results can be extraordinary. When you achieve those extraordinary results recognize why you achieved them and take care of the people who did that for you.

The third rule concerning bonuses is that it must be based on an objective measurement that the employee has major control or influence over.

What is an objective measurement? It is a measure that YOU don't control. Employees must feel that the actual results achieved will be reflected in the numbers on which the bonus is based. If you have any control or influence on the numbers, there will always be a suspicion that the numbers are "adjusted" to the benefit of the company and to the detriment of the employee. This feeling will exist, whether or not it is justified.

Determining the basis of a bonus plan is much more complex that it first appears. The first area for concern is that if an employee can achieve a bonus without the company achieving its goal, that is what will happen. The employee will try and increase his or her pay as high as possible with as little effort as possible. This is normal and it is the drive you are trying to tap into with the bonus plan. If your plan allows the employee to benefit without the company benefiting as a by-product, the plan, and not the employee performance, is to blame. To understand what I am trying to say let's use an example. In this example we will try and develop a bonus plan for the National Sales Manager of a company. His or her job is to sell, so it seems logical for the bonus to be based on actual sales achieved. Many companies do this, so how could it possibly be a problem?

Actually this is a problem. The problem occurs because additional sales are not the real objective of the company, additional profits are. Additional sales are simply one step, although a major step, in achieving the real goal, additional profits. We now have a situation where the goal of the company and the goal of the individual being compensated are not the same. The National Sales Manager is compensated for sales only, not profits. This situation will certainly lead to conflict and eventually the plan will break down. One effective way for this person to increase sales is to increase advertising and promotional expenses and extend higher discounts during the sales cycle. Both of these actions increase sales and thus increase the Sales Managers bonus but decrease profits for the company. The common way to control this is to require sales and promotional expenses to be budgeted and approved ahead of time. In this way a superior who has the interest of the company in mind can keep extraordinary expenses from occurring. In the same way, discounts could be passed through an approval process to prevent them from being used inappropriately.

Now, let's look at the mess we just created. The National Sales Manager has been told the company wants him or her to make as much bonus as possible but then makes it almost impossible to get necessary advertising and promotional efforts funded. The overseer believes the advertising levels are more than adequate, the National Sales Manager doesn't think its high enough at all. Just listen to him or her. "A huge personal effort is required just to get through the red tape required to place an ad. This effort should be directed toward actually selling the product instead of fighting the company I work for. When I need to make a snap decision to extend a small discount for an immediate order close, I can't do it because I have this stupid approval process to go through where I have to justify to people who have never sold anything, why I need to offer a particular discount to a particular customer. Sure I have a bonus plan but it isn't worth a damn because the company fights to keep me from achieving any real meaningful sales."

This isn't what we intended at all. This whole system has broken down because the bonus was poorly structured. If you want more profits, base the bonus on more profits and forget the bureaucracy. A properly structured bonus should require absolutely no controls or discipline. By itself, it should achieve a higher bonus for the employee when the real goal of the company is being achieved. In a properly structured bonus, an employee can only achieve personal success by making the company successful as a by-product.

In the example above, the bonus could be based on the margin from each sale. Margin in this example is the selling price of the product minus its direct manufacturing cost. From the margin, subtract the direct selling expenses such as advertising and promotion. Now base the bonus on the resulting number. Give advertising and promotion power to the Sales Manager. The Sales Manager must now balance discounts, which reduce margin and thus bonus with the need to close the sale. He or she must balance higher advertising expenses (ie. lower bonus) with the need for more new sales leads. No corporate control is needed. The Sales

Manager can allocate time as needed in the most efficient manner possible. We are now relying on the skills of the Sales Manager.

There is another, more subtle result from this program. Since both the level of sales and the manufacturing cost affect the Sales Manager's pay, he or she will have a real vested interest in how well the manufacturing operations are working. In fact, everyone whose bonus is based on profits will have this interest. They most certainly will express this interest to manufacturing management and will exert great pressure for the most efficient production possible. Pressure from peer workers has much more influence on most people than pressure from their boss. It's easy to hide things from the boss. It is impossible to hide things from your fellow workers.

This is an area for caution, however. There are many areas of discretionary expense that should not be subtracted from the bonus. For example, interest expense. In many companies, the balance between equity capital and borrowed money is a top management, shareholder or owner decision. If more of the company is sold off, equity capital is higher and there is less need to borrow money for normal operations. This means interest expenses are lower. If the decision is to keep the stock and operate on borrowed money, interest expenses are higher. In most companies none of the people within the company have any influence over this decision and thus they should not be penalized if the owners decide that higher interest expenses are best. There are other areas in the company that are similar. Including these types of expenses in the bonus calculation can derail and otherwise good plan so they should be very carefully considered when establishing the program.

People take very good care of their own money. Most people are much more careful and much more concerned with managing their own money than they are managing the company's money. This type of program makes their money and the company's money the same thing. Whenever an ad is placed, part of the money used to place the ad belongs to the employee. If the money wasn't spent, they could take home a slightly higher bonus. People are generally very careful about spending their own money. With this arrangement they will also be very careful about spending the company's money since the company's money and their money are the same thing.

This is probably the single most important part of running a new, highly efficient management structure. The bonus and motivational programs must be properly based so that each manager will do exactly what we want without any outside controls except the bonus program itself. If you must place any restrictions on the operation of the bonus program at all, it is not properly structured and I predict it will do your company more harm than good.

In most companies there are other factors that must be considered. This is especially true of slightly larger companies with somewhat more complex structures. Let us examine a company with several products and services. The common way to structure such a company is to separate it into several profit centers with a manager responsible for each area. I tend to support this type of structure since it focuses a manager on a specific product or service. When a manager is responsible for two or more product lines, each time they devote any resources to a product they have made a choice not to devote those resources to the other products they are responsible for. In this situation with a major bonus hanging on the results, any reasonable manager will focus on the products that promise the best immediate results with the least effort. They will "run with the winners" and generally ignore products that are not performing as well. New products tend to require significantly more effort than more established products. If they are grouped with existing, successful products, they might not receive the same level of attention as they would if someone's career was riding on its success or failure. Profit center divisions and individual product managers are ways of dealing with this situation. They are effective but carry with them the seeds of trouble.

If you set up a bonus program where each division manager is compensated for the profits of their own division, you create a situation where each division takes on the attitude of being a company of its own operating within the total corporation. Actions, which benefit one division at the cost of other divisions or the company as a whole, are viewed as totally acceptable.

If you set up a bonus program where each division head is compensated based on total company profits, division performance motivation is reduced somewhat, however, infighting between divisions is more likely. The better performing divisions will develop resentment toward the poorer performing divisions because they see those poor performers reducing their own pay and they can't do anything about it. Remember, these people are receiving a large part of their pay from these bonus programs. They will feel very strongly about them.

One system that I have successfully used and that I know works, is to base division bonuses on division profits minus shared corporate overhead. Take the profit developed by each division and subtract from that their share of the overall corporate overhead not directly associated with the division. Allocate the corporate overhead at the ratio of sales of one division to another. For example, if one division has sales double that of another division, it also must accept twice the corporate overhead. Let's see how this actually works.

Imagine you are a division manager in this situation. How do you increase your division profit and thus your bonus? Obviously the most direct way is to make more profit. Sell more. Develop some special sales incentives and sell more product. But, wait a minute. If you sell more without appropriate profit on those additional sales, you are actually worse off than if you didn't sell those extra products. The additional sales will subject you to a higher overhead allocation. If you don't make enough on the extra sales to cover that extra corporate overhead they could actually reduce your overall profitability and bonus. Sales for sales sake doesn't make sense. New sales must generate new profits or you will lose ground.

Another way to increase profits is to have the other divisions sell more. Higher sales in other divisions will mean that they absorb more overhead expense, reducing your overhead allocation and increasing your profits. It makes sense to do anything possible to help the other divisions increase sales, short of reducing your own division's profit. Another way to help the bonus is to campaign for lower corporate overhead. Any reductions you can make in corporate overhead levels will directly benefit you. Certainly you must review any planned increases in corporate overhead very carefully to make certain that they don't affect you negatively.

Just look at the above attitudes. They are exactly what you want from your managers and they occur naturally because of the structure of the bonus program. I can think of no other set of rules, procedures or management style that will yield the same result. This is also an extremely easy organization to manage. It requires little or no intervention by top management. Managers are internally motivated to do the proper thing without the need for someone to stand over them watching and guiding every move.

Structuring the bonus plan is the absolute keystone of an aggressive, competitive company. Spend a great deal of time thinking about and openly discussing the plan structure. Put yourself in place of each of the people affected by the plan and then imagine what you could do to increase your bonus. Try and imagine how you would feel about the other people and other divisions as the company goes through changes in business fortunes. Imagine one product and then another becoming successful and then losing favor. See and imagine how each of the people would feel as this occurs. Try and determine what actions they would take and see if that is what you want. Adjust the basic structure until you are very comfortable with the actions that people will likely take in response to the program.

The attitude you display as you introduce the program is very important. I don't think it makes any sense to launch the program with a great deal of fanfare. If it turns out to have problems, it is then much more difficult to adjust the terms of the program if those same terms were praised and touted at a formal high-energy introduction party. I believe it is better to ease the program into your organization rather quietly. When you first introduce the program, do it tentatively. Indicate that you will make changes during the first year or so until the program results in the management actions and reactions you want. If the program is properly structured it will motivate by itself. It should not require additional motivation from a strong introduction.

The bonus programs we have been talking about up to this point are aimed toward management people. Now, we should also consider the hourly paid production people. Attitudes here are different than with management. Management is paid to do a job. Sometimes that job can be done in 40 hours a week. Other times it may take substantially longer and at times it may be done in less time. An aware competitive company will recognize this and will allow some flexibility in working time. This type of management is officially called "exempt salaried". This means that these employees are exempt from the wage and hour laws governing overtime pay. There are specific legal requirements for a job that is considered "exempt". In general, if the job involves producing a product or processing paperwork associated with producing a product it cannot be "exempt". Only real management positions where planning and managing is the vast bulk of the work can be classified as "exempt".

"Non-exempt" jobs are those where people are paid for their time at work rather than being paid to do a job. The work they do during the time they are being paid for is determined by someone else. Since they are not exempt from the wage and hour laws, minimum rate of pay and overtime pay are dictated by law. The difference is subtle but important. It also results in a substantially different attitude on the part of the employee.

This difference in attitude between "exempt salaried" and "non-exempt hourly paid" employees often results in a rift or gap between the two groups. Management feels that labor needs to "work harder" to help increase profits and labor feels that management is trying to take advantage of them at every opportunity. This wall is damaging to a company and to its competitive abilities. It exists at every company I have ever seen to one extent or another. In some companies it is a serious barrier, in others it is much less rigid. Because the basic approach to the job is different for each group and because this difference is mandated by law, I don't feel it is possible to completely eliminate the barrier in today's business environment. Therefore, we must try to minimize it to whatever extent possible.

To try and understand this barrier better we must examine the concept of job security. Without a job, most people are very insecure. They generally feel that if they could just get a job, their financial security would improve. Once they have a job, their next concern is keeping the job. A paycheck coming in on a regular basis provides a feeling of security, provided there is a reasonable expectation that it will keep coming in. Job security is the feeling that paychecks will continue into the foreseeable future. People will react strongly to anything that threatens their job security. After all, the instinct for survival is the strongest instinct in human beings and threats to job security brings that instinct into play.

As a general rule, I believe most people believe that they have much more job security than they really have. Also, they believe the real threat to their job security is the company they work for when, actually, the real threat comes from that company's competitors. Hourly paid employees, working in the production operation, will generally have a high level of job security. As you move up the organization, security becomes less as knowledge of the reality of the business world increases.

Over the years I have promoted many people from the hourly paid ranks through middle management, sometimes to top-level positions. There is a psychological shock, which occurs with the promotion that most people don't expect. As an hourly paid production worker with a generally high level of job security, management jobs are viewed as being even more secure. You are higher up in the company and you make more money and therefore should feel more secure and better. Once they are in the new job, they discover that they are actually less secure and less comfortable. This seems to happen to pretty well everyone. The unexpected insecurity is something many people can't overcome and live with. I have had several instances where people chose to return to their previous jobs rather than deal with the new and frightening feelings.

Some people believe that with a little time they will get used to the job and feel better. Actually, this really doesn't happen. This new level of insecurity doesn't go away. In the higher level job you never seem to feel as secure as you did before. If you remain in the job, eventually you get used to being less secure and you may not be frightened. It is very unlikely, however, that you will ever feel as secure as you did in the lower level job.

I have discussed this phenomenon with each person that I have promoted into management ranks from hourly ranks and knowledge that this is a normal, natural problem does seem to help. The problem is very real, however. It is one you will need to deal with if you want to move promising people up in the company.

For those that remain in the hourly paid ranks, you need to deal with the security issue if you wish to have a good working relationship. Let's try and see your company through your worker's eyes.

The average hourly paid worker feels that they work hard and earn every penny they are paid. They go home each evening and brag about the good job they did and how they are better workers than their counterparts. They talk about their victories and how they caught and corrected errors that others made. I have yet to run into a worker who thinks they didn't work very hard or that they are overpaid.

Do you or your first line supervision believe that every one of your workers is putting forth 100%? Probably not. Does the guy who you think isn't pulling his weight go home thinking he is doing a good job? Most likely, yes. So how can you think someone is doing a poor job and they think they are doing a good job? The most common reason is that your definition of a good job and their definition aren't the same. There is a communication problem at the most basic level.

Another reason may be that you like one employee more than another. A person with a pleasant personality and good attitude may be viewed as doing a good job while another person with a negative personality or irritating habits doing exactly the same quality and quantity of work may be viewed negatively. Can this really happen in your factory? Not only can it happen, it absolutely will happen. It is normal, it is human and if your people are human they will act this way. This can lead to serious problems if you leave any part of handling hourly paid employees to the personal discretion of your managers or supervisors. When this happen it is absolutely devastating, not only to the poor employees but also to the good employees. The fact that someone's subjective personal attitude can have an impact on your job adds a level of insecurity that many hourly paid employees can't handle.

If this situation continues, the workers may very well force management to be fair. This is the most common reason that a company gets unionized. Most people think that a company's workers unionize to get more pay. The real reason most get unionized is that the workers feel they are being treated unfairly and they feel that the situation will not get better by itself. Fair in this case is fair in the eyes on the hourly paid workers, not fair in the eyes of management. Management has a more complete knowledge of the business situation and thus feels fully justified in the actions they take. The workers, however, believe that they have been treated unfairly and no reason justifies that. The conflict is very real and must be addressed if you want to run an efficient, competitive company.

How do we handle this situation?

The first thing you must accept is that you will not have complete freedom to act in dealing with your hourly paid employees. You must give up absolute dictatorial control of your poor employees in order to provide the minimum level of security for your good people. If you structure the company so that the hourly paid employees feel that they are being treated fairly and that the possibility of being treated unfairly is remote, then you will also limit management's ability to do whatever they want whenever they want.

The best way to add structure and stability to the workforce is to develop a complete and comprehensive policy manual. This written document should address every area of employment and should indicate the responsibilities of employees and limitations to the power of management. It should address exactly how difficult situations such as discipline, reductions in workforce and promotions are to be handled.

Think of this manual as the inalienable rights of the employees. Just as a free, democratic society provides its people with certain rights, a company that wishes to harness the real power of its people must also give those people certain rights and protections. These rights give your people the protection they need to feel secure and it is within this secure feeling that they are willing to take the risks and try the new things that will eventually make the company more efficient and profitable. They know that they can't lose their jobs without going through a long and clearly defined procedure. They will have plenty of warning.

Every once in awhile, you find you have a real problem employee. Someone you would love to just fire and be done with. They will, without a doubt, hide behind these protections just as many criminals hide behind the protection that the constitution provides in our country. In this situation, you must work within the written word in your policy manual, regardless of the problems this causes you. Understand, you are not doing this for the problem worker. You are doing this for all of the other really good workers in your company. If you simply ignore the rules and dismiss the problem worker, you have solved one problem but created another, even bigger one. All your good people now realize that regardless of what protections you have written down, they can really be dismissed anytime you want. They have absolutely no protection. You have proven that with the employee you dismissed. They also realize they are working for a liar. You told them that these rules would be followed but the first time you were faced with a difficult situation you abandoned the rules and did what you wanted.

If, on the other hand, you work within the rules, following the written procedure exactly, you will get some real benefit. All your good folks know that the person causing you problems is a real problem himself. They can see that you want to simply fire the jerk, but that instead you are following the rules that protect them. They realize that these rules really do work, even if in this case they are protecting someone that shouldn't be protected. Problem people eventually step over the line and you can get them. You can do it working within the rules and keep the rest of your people secure and working toward the important goals.

Developing this policy manual is not a trivial task. It will require much effort from you and your staff. Every area must be considered and discussed and eventually agreed upon. Don't underestimate the importance of this effort, however. Once complete, it will become a vital part of your company's ability to compete.

Once established, all management and supervision must follow the policy manual. It is the guidebook. A complete copy of the manual should be available for all employees to refer to and a condensed copy of the manual should be printed and provided to all employees.

The written procedures must be applied to all employees in exactly the same manner. The people you like and the people you don't like must be treated exactly the same. This is the key to providing the level of security needed to get real performance from your employees.

Doesn't this seriously limit the options of management? Also, won't it benefit those poor employees who constantly "walk the line" between acceptable and unacceptable performance or attendance? Yes it does and yes it will.

The employees who really take advantage of this program will tend to be those with the poorest performance. Frustration will build as you are forced to go through a structured disciplinary procedure instead of just firing them on the spot. Is it really worth the effort?

To help defend my position there is another point you must consider. You should realize that you don't really have the power to fire someone "on the spot" anyway. Certainly not in today's world. With the proliferation of laws to protect workers, you can be certain that any quick firing will be followed by an equally quick law suite. Without a clear and definite policy for firing, you may find it quite expensive to just fire someone because they did something wrong. You may even be forced by the courts to pay the person back pay, punitive damages and give them their job back. This, however is not the primary reason for the written procedures.

The real reason for this effort is your really good workers who will likely never be subject to discipline. If they see someone make a mistake and then get fired, they realize that they could also make a mistake and lose their jobs. This makes them very insecure even though they are extremely good people and would most likely never have a problem. On the other hand, if they see poor workers protected by the system and they see management following procedures they realize that it takes a pattern of ongoing problems to get fired. They know that they could possibly make a major error but they also realize that a single problem won't cost them their jobs. They tend to feel much more secure in this environment.

Another advantage of the written policy manual is that it becomes the "scapegoat" when something unpleasant must be done. It is the "policy" which must be followed and not the current desire of management. It provides a way of getting through difficult times while minimizing the negative impact on management, labor relations.

The key concept in this entire exercise is to substitute an objective set of rules and policies for the subjective and inconsistent actions of management. Your workers don't trust you to manage them in a consistent and fair manner. They would rather rely on a set of written policies. This is a reasonable reaction and, to some extent, it is justified. You and your management team are under a great deal of business pressure and, without a firm set of guidelines and rules, you will be inconsistent in handling your people. This is normal and natural. The actions you take will seem totally correct from your perspective. Your employees however, will view them from a totally different perspective. The written rules do generate a new set of constraints and do limit your management options. This does make the management job somewhat more difficult, however, it is the lesser of two evils. If you don't act in a fair and even handed manner you will need to deal with difficult relations with your production workers and the effort required to handle this situation will be much greater than living within a set of rules which you yourself set up.

The labor relations area is one of the few areas in business that I believe benefits from the use of an outside consultant. The labor relations consultants I have worked with have generally been very knowledgeable. They also bring to the relationship a type of third party credibility that management just doesn't have with their employees. Management can assure their people that in order to be totally fair we have brought in an objective expert to help refine the management labor relationship. These people can also assist in developing pay grades and formal job evaluations. These are all areas of extreme emotional content and having an outside consultant to lean on or to blame can be very helpful.

When we talked about management jobs, we discussed flexible job descriptions with overall goals driving the organization. With hourly paid production workers, job descriptions are generally more formal and somewhat less flexible. The more conventional structure is necessary to provide both control and stability needed for a secure environment. This does not mean that the organization is stiff or unyielding. It must balance the structure and stability needed for job security with a willingness to change when needed. Achieving this is a balancing act. Understanding what you are trying to accomplish will go a long way toward achieving the goal, however.

In dealing with the production organization, the first mind-set you should develop is that everyone is working to full capacity. The first step in achieving this is to hire the best, most dedicated people you can find. A little extra effort in the hiring process will be rewarded many times over. Even with the best people, every employee is not working to full capacity every day, but in general, people do try and do a good job and this fact should become the basis for your relationship with your production workers. This attitude indicates clearly that additional productivity cannot be achieved by working harder since people are already performing at full capacity. In almost every organization I have seen, this is the case. Sure, you can push harder for a short period of time and achieve more but you cannot reasonably expect to maintain that level over the long term.

This attitude then eliminates the need for motivational posters and slogans. If you think about it, a motivational poster encouraging workers to put forth more effort is a direct insult. It assumes that they are not currently putting forth full effort and that the company could sure benefit if they just did their job right. This core attitude on the part of management, which is very common in industry today, will totally undermine any efforts to tap into the ideas and knowledge of your production workers.

Getting your production people to use their minds and ideas as well as their bodies is the real goal. In addition to direct production labor, you want an ongoing flow of ideas and suggestions from your production people. During the last ten to fifteen years the idea of allowing production people to participate in management has become popular. Various programs have been developed including quality circles, participative management, and employee management teams. These have been used by many companies with varying degrees of success. Nonetheless, I disagree with the basic premise of many of these programs. They assume that the hourly paid employees can make management decisions as well or better than management. This is simply not true. In most companies if an employee is capable of a management position they have a management position. The production employees can, however, have a positive influence on management of the company. The production workers do have detail knowledge which management doesn't have. They have ideas that could be very useful. This knowledge can be vital to the success of new initiatives.

By "new initiative" I mean programs designed to produce a new product, change a production process or reduce costs. Most companies have these type of programs, some are successful, others not successful. Some take a great deal of "fixing" to finally get them working correctly. If you examine your new programs, both the successful and unsuccessful ones, you will find that those that were unsuccessful generally failed because some key component was unknown when the program started. To be more accurate, the components were unknown to management or to the people designing or running the program. Most likely, the production workers knew this critical information. They were simply not part of the program so they were not able to tell anyone about the potential problems so the program failed. In most cases they were not even aware that a program was being considered until it was implemented. At that point it was too late.

Production workers can affect a new program in other ways. If for some reason they do not support the program they can make it almost impossible for the new initiative to succeed. If they are part of the program they must support it or at least not be strongly opposed to it. Without their support, a new program will be quite difficult to successfully implement. Some programs simply fail because they do not have the support of the production people. Involving the production people can address both problems. It can discover the hidden traps and gain support from the production people, but it must be done correctly to work.

Most production people are afraid to speak out. Most companies have a few hourly workers who are outspoken but most workers try and keep their head down and do their job, drawing as little attention to themselves as possible. In this situation if you listen at all you will get the knowledge and opinion of just a couple of people which is normally not sufficient.

The goal is to try and develop channels where the less outspoken people can get their ideas and suggestions considered and implemented without drawing undue attention to themselves. Many of your people with excellent ideas are not interested in being a hero. Their motivation for providing suggestions is to make their job easier or to correct an obvious problem or to make the company better. Establishing a structure that seeks out these ideas without undue or uncomfortable attention is a delicate and somewhat difficult task.

Formal suggestion programs, which many larger companies conduct, are seldom successful. First, the employee must commit totally to their idea. They must then write it down and submit it to management. If it is implemented, they may receive a great deal of attention and perhaps a monetary reward. They will also be condemned by the other workers who had the same idea but didn't submit it. Overall, even a successful program will have an impact on most production workers that they will perceive as negative. If it does not work they will feel like a failure and will feel like they lost face with management reducing their chances for future advancement. Overall these programs will be regarded as very dangerous to ones career.

Real productivity advancement will come from hundreds or thousands of simple ideas not from a few well-documented "suggestions". To bring these ideas out you must foster an environment where all ideas are considered and any idea with a chance of success is tried. If it fails, it is abandoned with little fanfare. If it succeeds, it is adopted, also with little fanfare. This provides a method for production workers to affect their production environment without drawing undue attention. When sharing ideas is encouraged with the understanding that to be successful we must figure out ways to "work less" and still get the product out, this approach will pay huge dividends.

For this type of program to work, it must not involve middle or upper management until the idea is tried and is successful.

Unsuccessful attempts should be reversed and quietly forgotten without any publicity. In this way, people's egos are protected from failure and they are encouraged to express ideas more openly.

In an actual working structure, first line supervision, such as the production foreman should be trained to seek out these ideas and try them along with the production people. Most production people are comfortable with their foreman and if the foreman can be encouraged to approach new ideas with an open mind, a powerful synergy can develop. Working together they can try various ideas and adopt those that offer a real benefit. Attention is drawn to the programs only when they are successful, so there is little downside risk associated with openly expressing new ideas.

The real power of this approach lies in the power it gives to the production workers. My experience has shown that the average production worker is not particularly interested in glory or in standing out. They are, however, very interested in anything that affects their jobs. This system allows them to positively affect their jobs without having to draw undue attention to themselves. Once they realize and accept that the system does work, they have a low-risk tool that they can use to solve their own individual production problems. As different ideas are tried and the successful ones implemented, the small improvements brought about add together to become significant productivity improvements. The improved productivity should result in higher profits. The improved systems also result in improvement in employee jobs in many cases allowing them to accomplish more with less effort. If you have implemented a profit bonus program, the personal gain plus the improved working conditions helps reinforce the production improvement program encouraging even more effort to further improve the operation.

It is naïve to believe that this type of program can work without conflict. One person's idea may negatively affect another person. Some people may try and blame others when their ideas don't work as they expected. Conflict will be part of any program of this type and it must be dealt with. The effort required to deal with the conflict is normally much less than the rewards realized from the effort.

The overall goals must be constantly restated and used to measure the progress and success of the various programs. Ideas or programs must not take on a life of their own but must be cast as tools to achieve the overall goal. They should be given no intrinsic value of their own. Only the overall goals should be given real value. The new ideas or tools are used as long as they function and then should be discarded with little fanfare when they no longer work.

Ultimately, someone must be the final judge and final authority. This final authority makes the tough decisions and those decisions become law. This authority should not be overused. It should be kept in the background for use in rare occasions when fundamental conflict must be resolved. The goal should not be to eliminate conflict. A certain amount of conflict is healthy, however, when it becomes too intense it must be resolved by edict. Without a final authority to resolve runaway conflict, this type of program can deteriorate into chaos with different factions and different ideas all being promoted with equal vigor. In this type of totally unstructured environment, progress is difficult because everyone isn't pulling in the same direction.

For the program to be ultimately successful there must be a final power, a final authority that is both able and willing to make final decisions. Under this authority should exist a great deal of freedom, provided chaos doesn't develop and the overall result is progress. This is a bit of a balancing act, but can be highly effective and highly profitable when it works correctly. The power structure and authority provide some security and stability while the freedom provides the ability to experiment and make things better.

A good example of this was my company's latest plant expansion. Production layout is normally an engineering effort. In this case, we decided to have the production people and production management develop the layout themselves. We did not have them develop a plan and then have top management review and approve it. Instead, they developed and approved the plan themselves and did not even tell top management what they were doing. They installed the systems, modified whatever they thought was needed and within a few months they had evolved a highly efficient production environment. They were happy, management was happy and it was all completed with little or no conflict. I seriously doubt that this would have been as successful if top management had been involved.

Your people are your single most valuable asset. Over the years I have observed that most companies severely underutilize this resource. Managers use their subordinates as extensions of their own ability rather than as additions to themselves. They control every aspect of their people's jobs carefully directing each and every decision. By managing in this manner, their own limitations become limitations of all of their people. The entire team must then suffer the limitations of its leader. This carefully managed team performs to only a fraction of its potential because of, what I believe is a serious flaw in the team manager.

In a highly competitive market, this rigidly managed team doesn't stand a chance against a team where individuals are allowed more freedom to perform against a set of clear goals. The fundamental difference between these two management approaches lies in the manager's attitude toward his or her subordinates. If the manager is convinced that he or she is the most knowledgeable and skilled person on the team and that all other members are inferior and must be guided, then rigid control of all operations seems the correct path. If the team leader believes that each member of the team is most skilled and most knowledgeable in their own individual jobs and that the team leader has the greatest knowledge of the overall direction and goals, then a much more enlightened and effective management style will occur. The difference between these two attitudes is very subtle and very important.

It is somewhat like the coach of a professional sports team. The coach understands the game, the strategy and the capabilities and limitations of the players. The coach, however, cannot play the game as well as the players. The coach sets the directions and guides the team, but the real skill is with the players who actually have to play the game.

The rigidly controlled team will perform well in most markets provided they are competing against other rigidly controlled teams. In this competitive situation, the most disciplined most carefully controlled team will generally prevail. When these highly structured teams must compete against teams operating to the full potential of all of their members, it isn't even a good contest. The rigid team experiences frustration after frustration as their higher cost lower capability effort runs into a highly efficient, flexible competitor operating at lower cost. Every aspect of the competition favors the openly managed competitor.

This book is about surviving and competing in the new millennium. A hard driving team of motivated people is an important ingredient to achieving this goal. The key to generating this team is not in selecting the "perfect" people or even in defining and communicating the corporate direction and goals. The key is in designing the compensation and bonus programs so that when people are given freedom to perform, they achieve the overall corporate goals. They do not achieve these goals by following directions dictated by management. Instead, they achieve these goals by working diligently to maximize their own personal compensation. In fact, the goal of everyone in the company should be to maximize everyone's compensation. If the compensation programs are structured properly, the corporate goals will occur, not as the primary objective but instead as a by-product of the effort to improve personal compensation.

People will put forth drive, commitment and energy for their own personal goals well beyond the efforts they are willing to put forth for the company. By structuring the company so that the work they do and the success generated by that work directly benefits them, you can tap into this energy. The result is a team and a company that is almost impossible to beat.

This approach makes an assumption that might not be obvious on the surface. That assumption is that the consensus decisions of all the people in the company will be best for the company. It also implies that the consensus management is superior to obtaining direction for a few skilled managers. Are these assumptions true?

To answer that question, I will end this chapter with a story about an experiment conducted at a computer conference. At this conference, they equipped several thousand seats with a set of aircraft controls. On a large projection monitor in front of the audience, they projected the control panel and forward view from a Boeing 747 airliner. Using a real 747 simulator, they placed the aircraft in the air and told the audience to land at a specific airport. The input to the simulator was the average of the input of all the seats in the audience.

It is very likely that no single person in the audience was capable of accomplishing this task. The people conducting the experiment had no idea of the outcome. This was a great way to see if the combined skill of the audience was better than that of a single individual.

The result was almost dull. The aircraft flew directly to the airport and made a perfect approach and landing.

This teaches us an important lesson but there is more.

Two years later, the experiment was repeated. This time, the controls were a bit more complex. The machine was an undersea mining machine. The audience was told to move around the ocean bottom and pick up nodules that were lying on the ocean bottom. Controls included not only the ability to move around but also the ability to control a robotic arm that was used to pick up the nodules.

When the experiment started, nothing happened. The mining machine remained stationary. It didn't move for forty five minutes. People were shouting at each other and there was a general state of chaos but it was obvious that everyone was trying to move in a different direction and so nothing happened.

After forty five minutes, one of the experiment directors made a single statement using the microphone and the machine began to move. It then efficiently picked up the nodules.

What did he say?

All he said was "Why don't you go right."

These are great stories because they demonstrate the dynamics of the consensus management that I am recommending for future furniture companies. Many managers will not like the conclusion but, without a doubt, your people, properly motivated and working together can manage the details of running the company better than you can. To do this, however, the second experiment showed that a clear direction is absolutely necessary. The consensus group can't operate without someone providing a direction.

As I wrote this book, I questioned whether I should delve into this area, which is somewhat removed from the technical aspects of Furniture Fabrication. Although I felt that furniture fabrication could function in a traditionally managed company, I also decided that to be truly competitive, furniture companies would eventually need to adopt advanced management techniques. For most people these ideas are not that easy to accept and some will never accept them. At the same time, I felt that it was important to at least get the concepts into print where they can be discussed and debated. I decided to include this chapter.

# INDEX

# Index